BE PLASTIC CLEVER

BE PLASTIC CLEVER

BY AMY & ELLA MEEK

Foreword by **STEVE BACKSHALL**

DK | Penguin
Random

First published in Great Britain in 2020 by
Dorling Kindersley Limited
80 Strand, London, WC2R 0RL

A CIP catalogue record for this book
is available from the British Library.
ISBN: 978-0-2414-4707-9

Printed and bound in Great Britain by
Clays Ltd, Elcograf S.p.A.

A WORLD OF IDEAS:
SEE ALL THERE IS TO KNOW

www.dk.com

FSC

CONTENTS

Make a change

Being an activist

The future

Get started

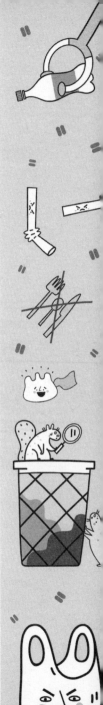

FOREWORD

By Steve Backshall

I started my first conservation TV series with National Geographic back in 1999, when mobile phones were the size of bricks and some TV's were still **black and white!** Back then, environmental themes felt new. Many of our shows uncovered completely new science about the effect of humans on climate change, habitat loss, wildlife extermination, and the looming threat of plastic pollution. Even for a naturalist like me, the revelations were new and shocking. The world expert scientists we filmed with always concluded by saying things like:

"THE SCIENCE IS IN, WE KNOW THIS IS HAPPENING AND HOW TO DEAL WITH IT, THE TIME IS NOW, WE HAVE TO ACT OR IT WILL BE TOO LATE".

Sound familiar? In the following decades, those words have become like a mantra to the conservation community and now finally **the sixth extinction** has entered the common lexicon. And not a moment too soon. There has been a noticeable rapid decline in the state of our diverse environments in just the last three or four years. Inevitably if I find a deserted tropical beach hundreds of miles from civilisation, the strand line will look like a rubbish dump, with bottles, diapers, straws, current-borne flotsam, and discarded jetsam. On a beach in Gabon, West Africa, we found **bottles** from China, **bags** from Brazil, **aerosol cans** from Indonesia, and a **baby potty** from the UK! Once discarded, our plastic garbage becomes a global problem.

On every SCUBA dive I do nowadays I need to carry twine cutters – I've had to use them to cut loose seals, sharks, fish, coral heads, and turtles from nets and indestructible plastic trash. As I write this, my beloved Australia is on fire, with a loss to wildlife and nature that cannot be quantified. Amy and Ella's generation have grown up with these looming concerns as an omnipresent spectre over their futures. **The sixth extinction** is to them, what **Chernobyl** and the **Cold War** were to me as a kid; just as scary, every bit as insidious, with the potential outcome every bit as cataclysmic.

I first met the (far from) Meek Sisters when they spoke before a lecture I was giving at the **Royal Geographical Society**. They were no more than 14 and 12, and the audience was blown away by their poise and eloquence, outperforming their adult counterparts (very much including me). While there were already many young conservationists making a name for themselves by speaking from the heart with passion and emotion, what impressed me about this pair was that they fact-checked everything they said with peer-reviewed science. These weren't just feisty firebrands that might burn bright then fade away. They were in it for the long haul. And all of a sudden, I find that I'm following in **THEIR FOOTSTEPS**, speaking alongside them in Parliament, appearing on their TV show, pinching their experiments and results for my own lectures – watching their inevitable, inexorable maturation into world-class conservationists.

Amy and **Ella** give me **HOPE.** They have drive, awareness, and purpose, in a way I never had. They and their contemporaries believe they can change the world. We have to believe they are right. This time in history, for all its madness, will be looked back on and equated to the great civil rights movements of the past. As a time when young people stood up and shouted about what they believe in – the future of our planet and all life upon it. Ella and Amy will be leaders in that movement, and I am proud to know them.

Steve Backshall

HI! We're Amy and Ella from
KIDS AGAINST PLASTIC

I'm Amy, the author of this book

We're really pleased that you've found our book and, more importantly, that you're keen to do your bit to help save the planet! After all, there's only one Earth so we best take care of it.

Just before we start, we'd like to quickly clear something up. Our campaign is called Kids Against Plastic, but that doesn't mean that we're against **ALL** plastic. That would be a bit daft, especially because of how reliant we all are on plastic, whether we like it or not. Instead, we are focused on tackling **single-use plastics** – the convenience items we use once for just minutes before leaving them to persist in the environment forever. Anyway, more on that later.

We're guessing that you've probably already heard that plastic pollution is becoming a really big problem for us humans. We've created an environmental disaster that is quickly spiralling out of control. Our beautiful, picture-postcard locations – beaches, rivers, and national parks – are becoming covered in a blanket of plastic waste. We're hearing scary facts in the news about how by 2050 there'll be **more plastic in the oceans than fish**, and almost on a daily basis we're seeing the impact of plastic on animals and wildlife. You've seen the photos of whales, turtles, and seabirds washing up on beaches around the world dead, with their stomachs stuffed full of plastic, right? And the chances are, if you've eaten fish, mussels, or crab recently, you've probably swallowed some microscopic pieces of plastic in the process!

You see, the important thing to remember about plastic pollution is that it's not an issue that only concerns beach dwellers, sea life, or people living near rivers; it affects **EVERYONE**, even if sometimes invisibly. And, it's an issue that **EVERYONE** is contributing to. Sometimes unknowingly, like when we flush microfibres from our washing machines into the waterways, or by visibly littering in the environment. We'd bet that you've probably encountered plastic waste before in your life: in the form of plastic bottles thrown onto motorway verges or plastic cups scattered across festival fields. Whether we like it or not, plastic is in all our lives, for the better or worse. It's something we can all see before us, can touch, and sometimes even smell – yuk! And plastic pollution not only stinks, it's ugly to look at. No one likes to walk through their local park and see bags in the trees or wrappers on the ground.

I'm Ella!

But perhaps the scariest bit about plastic pollution is the fact that at the rate things are going, us kids, and other generations of kids, are going to be **the ones who will have to clear it up**. We're going to inherit this problem because of one of plastic's most incredible properties: it is durable and lasts practically forever. The average plastic straw takes 200 years to break down – and even then it still remains in the form of tiny plastic fragments. It takes ages to go away. This means that when we're adults, all the plastic rubbish we currently see on land and in the sea will still be somewhere on the planet. Almost **EVERY** piece of plastic ever made still exists on the Earth today, so there's a heck of a lot of it. We're the ones who are going to have to deal with the mess left by our parents and grandparents.

Over the years Ella and I have been campaigning as part of our charity Kids Against Plastic, and the question we're most commonly asked is: **how can we stop this?** How can we, as the younger generation of this world, actually make a difference and have our voices heard? How can you help? We hope this book will serve as the answer.

One of the unique things about plastic pollution as an environmental problem is the fact that it is something that everyone can respond to themselves. No one can argue that plastic pollution doesn't exist, and everyone can do their bit to clean up their local area, whether it's picking up rubbish from local

streets or carrying a reusable mug for hot drinks. This means that **YOU** can do the same. This book is here not only to inform you about plastic pollution and climate change, but also to help you find your voice. It's here to help you shout about the issues you're passionate about.

Hopefully, this book will help you to make the change you've always wanted. Kids have huge potential, but we don't often realise it. We're so often told to **"sit down and be quiet"** that it's easy to forget that we have a voice – and an important, powerful one at that. If we put our minds to something, we can make big changes happen. With so many environmental campaigners being adults or large organisations, it's just as important that us kids have a voice too.

Afterall, we are the future, but we are also the present. If we want change to happen at the speed and scale needed, we have to make it happen, or the environmental legacy we leave will not be the pristine one we imagine.

Amy and Ella Meek

1

PLASTIC PROBLEMS

We all contribute to plastic pollution in lots of ways, from food packaging to how we dispose of our waste. This makes it hard to know where to start, as it's such a big issue! But don't worry, a large part of finding a solution comes from understanding the problem, so let's find out a bit more about plastic pollution.

Introducing the
PLASTICS

To get started, let's clarify some of the types of plastic.
Simply speaking, there are many types of plastic with a variety of different properties and uses, and to try to cover them all in a short book would be **practically impossible** – and make for a pretty boring read!

So, throughout this book, we'll mainly be concentrating on single-use plastics – plastic items that are used once and thrown away soon after. They are sometimes called **convenience plastics**. You've probably heard of them – they are getting a lot of attention these days due to their negative impact on the environment.

In an ideal world, or even just a world free of plastic pollution, it would be tempting to say, "Ban all single-use plastic!"

But, unfortunately, it's not that simple. There are lots of complications that make it hard to get rid of plastic. How annoying!

To help you get your head around this, we're going to take you through **THREE DIFFERENT CATEGORIES OF SINGLE-USE PLASTIC**.

Essential

Can you imagine walking into a hospital and seeing no plastic at all? No plastic-wrapped medical equipment, no plastic drip bags hooked up to patients, no single-use scrubs for surgery? Let's face it, you wouldn't want to go into hospital for an operation and see the doctors unwrapping paper bags of medical instruments.

IN PLACES LIKE HOSPITALS, PLASTIC IS THE PERFECT MATERIAL TO USE! It's necessary for sealing items that need to be completely clean for long periods of time, like hospital equipment. This is something that paper could never do. And this means that sometimes, plastic is a necessity – that is, until we find a suitable alternative (fingers crossed). Even plastic straws can fall into this category, as people with medical conditions sometimes need plastic straws to be able to eat. These are what we class as **essential plastics** – they're needed for their purpose and it's hard to use alternatives.

Avoidable

So now we've got the essentials covered, it's on to the avoidable plastics. These are the ones that we have problems with – **BECAUSE THEY ARE THE PROBLEM!** These types of plastic make up the single-use items we see so often, like plastic coffee cups and drinks bottles. And the reason that these items are BIG problems where plastic pollution is concerned is because we are pretty stupidly using a material that lasts almost forever, to make items that we use for just a few minutes before we throw them away.

A PLASTIC BOTTLE LASTS FOR UP TO 450 YEARS and even then, it only breaks down into tiny pieces called **microplastics.** These microplastics don't easily break down, which means that they stay around polluting the planet for thousands of years! That's a lot of problems that could be avoided pretty easily by just using reusable items instead.

See you later

Sure!

20

Hard-to-replace

Plastic is, in many ways, the perfect material,
particularly when it comes to food packaging.
We're not just talking about how lightweight and
cheap it is, plastic also allows perishable foods – ones
that go off, such as bread and vegetables – to be
preserved for longer in airtight packaging.

This means that for supermarkets and
companies that supply them with goods,
plastic is by far the winner when deciding
how to package their products. For
example, cucumbers only last for a few
days when sold loose, but when they're
wrapped in plastic film, they can last for up
to two weeks! It also means that most
supermarkets see banning plastic altogether
as a bad idea until a suitable alternative is found.

Those cucumbers
don't stand a
chance!

A brief HISTORY of PLASTIC

1839
American Charles Goodyear discovers that adding a fine powder called **sulphur** to **natural rubber** strengthens it. This process makes rubber suitable for tyres.

1856
English inventor Alexander Parkes creates **Parkesine**, the first human-made plastic. It's used to make objects including combs and cutlery handles.

1907
Belgian-American chemist Leo Baekeland invents **Bakelite**. It is the first plastic made **ENTIRELY** from synthetic, or artificial, components.

1935
American chemist **Wallace Carothers** invents the silky plastic **nylon** for the company DuPont.

1931
Polystyrene begins to be manufactured in Germany.

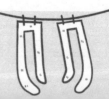

For many years, plastic was seen as a miracle material, much lighter and more versatile than **wood**, **glass**, **ceramics**, and **metal**, and often just as strong. It's only in recent years that we've begun to see the bad side of plastic. We've started to become aware of how much of a problem our overuse and over-reliance on plastic is, and how it impacts the natural world.

1959

Swedish engineer Sten Gustaf Thulin develops the first lightweight plastic **shopping bag** – hoping that it would help save trees!

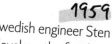

1950s

"Throwaway living" using **single-use plastics** is celebrated as a sign of progress in the modern world.

2004

Marine biologist Richard Thompson coins the word "**microplastics**" to describe the tiny pieces of plastic that pollute the oceans, rivers and lakes, soil, and air.

1948

Tupperware, a company that makes household plastic containers, is launched in the United States.

2020

Yearly production of plastic is at more than 300 million tonnes (331 million tons).

STRANGE and DIFFERENT

Plastic pollution doesn't just come in the form of plastic bottles. Here are a few different, and surprising, types of plastic waste we find contaminating the environment.

Nurdles

These are tiny, white plastic "pearls" – pellets of raw plastic that are melted down and shaped into the products we see on shelves. Sometimes, ships carrying these nurdles can lose a container or two overboard during rough weather, and suddenly millions and millions of these plastic nuggets are lost to the sea. This happened to a freight ship travelling across the South China Sea in 2012, and beaches on nearby coastlines are still covered in nurdles that wash up every high tide.

Car tyres

According to a study by Friends of the Earth, up to 19,000 tonnes of microplastic pollution are entering UK waterways every year from vehicle tyres, which shed tiny particles that float down drains, as well as contributing to air pollution. That's gross enough but it gets worse – we can end up inhaling the tyre particles! Tyres are believed to be responsible for the greatest proportion of microplastic entering European waters.

Toys

Have you ever accidentally stepped on a plastic toy with bare feet – **OUCH right?** It's bad enough at home – can you imagine doing the same at the beach? Okay, plastic toys aren't one of the main forms of plastic pollution, but there have been instances when our lost, sea-faring toys turn up to litter our beaches.

In 1997, a container of plastic toys was lost from a ship at sea during a storm and pieces are STILL washing up on beaches, over 20 years later! There have even been cases where thousands and thousands of rubber ducks have washed ashore.

What a load of
GARBAGE!

In the open waters of the world's oceans, currents come together to form vast, slowly swirling areas called gyres.

There are six major gyres on the surface of Earth's oceans. These areas act like whirlpools to pull in waste washed into the sea from land or dumped from ships. Little was known about this kind of plastic pollution until 1997, when American Charles Moore sailed through a huge area of plastic debris during a race across the Pacific Ocean.

The waste isn't just floating on the water's surface. It is also spread out at different depths, all the way down to the ocean floor.

Garbage collects in gyres around the world.

North Atlantic Gyre

South Pacific Gyre

South Atlantic Gyre

Indian Ocean Gyre

These large areas of plastic debris became known as **"GARBAGE PATCHES"**. They are like vast floating islands made of pieces of plastic and tangled fishing nets. Plastic breaks down so slowly in water that it may never disappear completely.

The Great Pacific Garbage Patch

The biggest area of ocean rubbish is known as the Great Pacific Garbage Patch. It is around six times the size of the UK, and contains more than a trillion pieces of rubbish – most of which are plastic. It's extremely dangerous because animals mistake the plastic for food and get tangled up in the fishing nets.

North Pacific Gyre

Cleaning it up

In 2011, 16-year-old Boyan Slat was shocked to see more plastic than fish in the sea while diving in Greece. The Dutch student set about designing a clean-up system that would collect plastic drifting in ocean currents. In 2013 he founded the environmental organisation **THE OCEAN CLEANUP.** It's complicated to make the system effective, but it launched in 2019.

Dear Diary...

"Artivism"

Using art to support a campaign or promote a cause is a tried and tested approach. The idea is to create something that looks interesting or appealing at first glance – this is sometimes referred to as "eye candy" – but once looked at more closely, a deeper message is revealed.

The Monster of the Ocean

Ella and I were around 9 and 11 years old, I think, when we decided to build our Monster of the Ocean sculpture. It was a dangerous-looking sea reptile-y thing made from plastic that had been washed up onto a beach in North Yorkshire. I'm not even sure that we were that into plastic pollution at that point – I guess we were just fed up of seeing **plastic rubbish washed up on the beaches** where we liked to play. Oh, and the plan was to enter our sculpture into a competition being run by an ethical ocean-focused clothing company.

So, **we did a beach clean**, took the rubbish items we'd collected home and washed them all in a big dustbin full of soapy water. Then we started building and gluing the different objects together to create our piece of art. We had no idea what the Monster should look like, but we used a jaw-like piece of tubing as a starting point and just made it up from there. Eventually – tadah! – the final touches were completed and our **Monster of the Ocean** was ready to be taken back to its original habitat for a photoshoot. It was a metaphor for the threat of plastic to our oceans, and we were very happy with our "**ARTIVISM**" (art + activism = artivism).

Plastic irony in Brighton

A few years later, we had become much more aware of **plastic pollution**. So, after visiting an exhibition on ocean plastic at a museum in Brighton, we headed straight to the beach – fists clenched, feeling angry and determined – to see what state it was in. We found lots of what we would later start referring to as the **Big 4** (plastic cups and lids, straws, bottles, and bags), as well as large quantities of Nylon fishing line and netting.

We felt compelled to try to do our bit to raise awareness and took all of the rubbish we'd cleared up to the promenade. We used the discarded netting to create a mesh onto which we added bottle tops, bottles, and bags. The strings of lids and bottles we tied onto it rattled annoyingly against the metal railings – perfect! We chalked slogans and stats about plastic pollution onto the pavement.

As we walked away, we turned and looked proudly at our **artivism installation** – after all, we'd removed plastic that had been on that beach for years! The next day, however, we learned that the council had removed our installation. We were not happy at all, but were able to smile at the irony of the council only considering the plastic to be a nuisance once it was on the promenade, not when it was on the beach!

"Earth provides enough to sustain every man's NEED, but not every man's GREED."

Mahatma Gandhi

Mohandas Karamchand Gandhi (1869–1948), known as Mahatma ("Grand Soul"), was the leader of India's independence movement against British rule. His acts of non-violent resistance inspired civil rights movements across the world. Gandhi was a vegetarian, and campaigned against violence towards animals.

TYPES of plastic

Most plastic packaging has, on the back of it, a small triangle with a letter or a number written inside. These little symbols are easy to overlook, but are really important for knowing what to do with that piece of plastic when you're finished with it! They tell you what kind of plastic it is, out of seven main types.

PET

This is the plastic that you often see on supermarket shelves! It's used to make plastic bottles, biscuit trays, and the plastic jars we often see sauces or spreads packaged in.

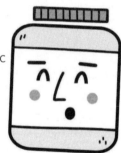

HDPE

HDPE is a stronger type of plastic. It is what milk bottles are made of, along with shampoo bottles and freezer bags.

PVC

You probably wouldn't see this on the supermarket shelves! PVC is often used to make piping and twines.

LDPE

LDPE is a very soft and flexible plastic. So, you'll often see it as squeezy bottles for things like ketchup, and as cling film.

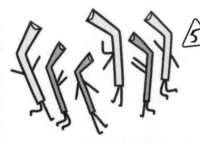

PP

This plastic is used for a range of everyday items, from straws and yoghurt pots to clothes hangers.

PS (POLYSTYRENE)

This plastic is pretty recognisable! You'll probably have seen it as those cheap white cups you get hot drinks in, or as takeaway food packaging.

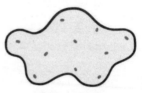

OTHER

Now, this is what it says on the tin. Type 7 encompasses all the other types of plastic, such as polycarbonate (used to make CDs) and acrylic (a plastic sometimes used instead of glass).

CONFUSING, RIGHT?

No wonder it's so hard to know what plastic you can and cannot recycle – we'll clear it up on pages 38–39!

Plastic
FOREVER...

One of plastic's **BEST** properties, but also its **WORST**, is how durable it is. Us humans have designed a material that's **practically indestructible**, which makes it perfect for items that we want to use for a long time. However, this is not so great when it comes to the environment, as plastic can stay in the same form for **hundreds of years**. Let's take a closer look at how long it takes different plastic items to break down...

Plastic bags
15-20 YEARS

Plastic straws
200 YEARS

I'm thin and tearable so it takes less time for me to decompose than something like a plastic straw. But, as I'm usually only used once, that's a long time to hang around!

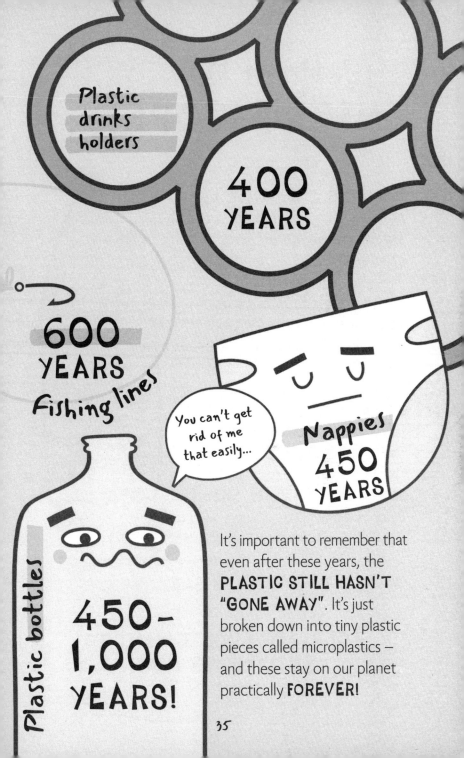

It's important to remember that even after these years, the **PLASTIC STILL HASN'T "GONE AWAY"**. It's just broken down into tiny plastic pieces called microplastics — and these stay on our planet practically **FOREVER!**

35

Under the
MICROSCOPE

Despite their differences, all plastics have one thing in common – they are all human-made materials, created from lots and lots of chemicals. You may have seen a big label on plastic or reusable bottles in the supermarket saying **"BPA Free!"**. That's because BPA – one of the chemicals used to make hard plastics for things like water bottles and food containers – is thought to be really bad for our health. Many experts say that BPA can interfere with hormones in our body, which are responsible for important functions such as growth and repair. BPA has also been linked to health problems including heart disease or diabetes (when your body struggles to manage the amount of sugar in your blood).

BPA FREE!

I CERTAINLY DON'T WANT TO BE DRINKING THAT!

BPA has, thankfully, had its use restricted in items for babies and young children in places including the EU, China, and Malaysia. However, many other chemicals in plastic can also be really bad for us if large amounts get into our bodies – and we may be drinking them without even knowing it!

Have you ever left your plastic bottle in the car for a while when it's hot? And the drink inside tastes really weird and disgusting? Well, what you're tasting are chemicals from the bottle that have leached into the liquid itself. To make it worse, scientists don't know what effect all these toxins will have on us in the long run. **EEEK!**

But, don't stress too much! These chemicals only become a big problem if we leave water in our bottles for a long time. Just make sure that if you're refilling a bottle, use a reusable one instead of a plastic bottle designed for one use!

What is RECYCLING?

At the moment, we produce a lot of rubbish that isn't recycled. Much of it ends up in useless, messy heaps on landfill sites, or gets burned – creating **smelly, toxic fumes**. Shockingly, only 9% of all the plastic that has ever been made is likely to have been recycled!

However, there's a simple plan you can follow to cut down on what you chuck away:

REDUCE

Try to lessen the amount of stuff you throw away. For example, you could use a **tote bag** to carry shopping instead of disposable plastic bags.

REUSE

Instead of throwing things in the bin after you've used them, think about **what else they could be used for.** Turn an old jam jar into a vase, or give your old toys to charity.

RECYCLE

If you can't reuse them, objects can be broken down into parts and made into something new. **This is called recycling.**

What can be recycled?

It can be difficult to figure out whether something can be recycled or not. Here are some plastic items that can be recycled, and some that can't. If you're not sure, check your local recycling guidelines online

✓ ✗

Polyethylene terephthalate (PET)
- Water bottles
- Fizzy drink
- bottles

Polystyrene (PS)
- Yoghurt pots
- Foam
- packaging

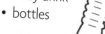

High-density polyethylene (HDPE)
- Milk bottles
- Shampoo bottles
- Washing-up liquid bottles

Low density polyethylene (LDPE)
- Carrier bags
- Squeezy bottles
- Packaging film
- Bin liners

The priority is to reduce your plastic use as this has the biggest impact. Turn to pages 101–102 for some tips on how to do this.

HOW IS
plastic recycled?

There are many steps to the plastic recycling process, and **it takes time and energy**. At the recycling centre, people sort through different types of plastic by hand before it is put through a series of machines that crush it, chop it up, clean it, melt it, chop it up again, and finally remould it into something new.

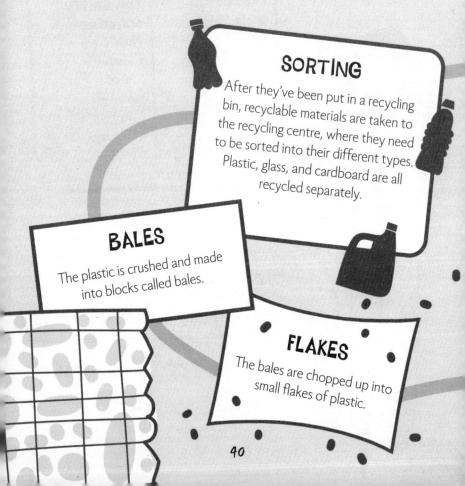

SORTING

After they've been put in a recycling bin, recyclable materials are taken to the recycling centre, where they need to be sorted into their different types. Plastic, glass, and cardboard are all recycled separately.

BALES

The plastic is crushed and made into blocks called bales.

FLAKES

The bales are chopped up into small flakes of plastic.

PLASTIC BOTTLES

Polyethylene terephthalate, or PET, is a type of recyclable plastic found in most plastic bottles.

PLASTIC PELLETS

PET pellets can be melted down and poured into moulds to make new objects, such as bottles.

MELTING AND CHOPPING

The PET flakes are melted. The liquid plastic hardens into a lump which is then chopped into pellets.

CLEANING

Water separates the PET from parts that can't be recycled. The heavy PET sinks. Labels, and other bits that can't be recycled, float upwards.

RECYCLING around the WORLD

It's sometimes hard to get people to recycle their rubbish, instead of just throwing it away. Different countries have come up with loads of creative ways to encourage people to recycle more. Here are just a few popular recycling schemes...

Plastic bottle deposit scheme, Sweden

In some countries, when you buy a drink in a plastic or glass bottle, or an aluminium can, you have to pay a little bit more. However, once you've finished drinking it, you can feed the bottle into a **recycling machine** and get this extra money back. Sweden has been running this scheme since the 1980s, with **85%** of bottles and cans being recycled in this way.

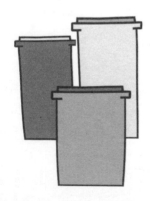

Colour-coded recycling bins, Germany

In Germany, there are six different types of recycling bins – **black** for general waste, **brown** for composting, **yellow** for plastic, **white** for clear glass, **green** for coloured glass, and **blue** for paper. Over the years, sorting rubbish this way has become second nature.

Top recyclers!

These are the countries that recycle the most waste:

GERMANY
56.1%

AUSTRIA
53.8%

SOUTH KOREA
53.7%

WALES
52.2%

SWITZERLAND
49.7%

Law and punishment, South Korea

There are very strict laws in South Korea surrounding the use of plastic in public places such as shops and restaurants. In August 2018, the government banned the use of plastic cups inside cafes. Businesses who disobeyed the rules would be fined 2 million won, which is more than **£1,000!** In January 2019, plastic bags were banned in all South Korean supermarkets.

RECYCLING and DOWNCYCLING

Most of us think that if we put a plastic item in the recycling bin, it will always get made into a new version of that item. Isn't that what we're often told by the companies that make our plastic-packaged products?

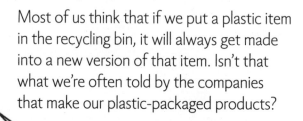

Unfortunately, particularly when it comes to disposable plastics, this isn't the case!

Often, the plastic that we put in the recycling bin is downcycled – this basically means it's broken down and made into items of lower quality than the original product.

A BOTTLE COULD BE MADE INTO SOMETHING LIKE A CARPET, OR EVEN A FLEECE!

This sounds like a **GREAT** solution, as we're making exciting new things from something as simple as a plastic bottle! But unfortunately, downcycling isn't actually as good as it seems. For a start, by creating new types of products it means that **EVEN MORE** plastic is needed, just to replace the millions of items we used the day before!

Also, the plastic fibres that are in our fleeces shed every time we put our clothes in the wash. These super tiny plastics are called **microfibres**, and are too small to be filtered, which means most of them wash straight from our washers into waterways, adding to plastic pollution even more. **EEEK!**

Lunchtime

MICROFIBRES

So, we know that lots of plastic is downcycled into clothes, and that this is contributing to plastic pollution through the release of microfibres into the environment. But let's look more closely at microfibres, and why exactly they are so bad.

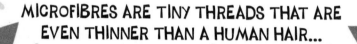

MICROFIBRES ARE TINY THREADS THAT ARE EVEN THINNER THAN A HUMAN HAIR...

Around 60% of material used to make clothing is plastic. Some of the most common plastics you'll see are polyester, nylon, and acrylic.

You can find out what your clothes are made from by looking at the tags. You'll see that lots of your clothes will be at least some part plastic!

Now, most facilities that manage our waste water are unable to filter microfibres out of the water because of their super small size. This means they wash straight into our rivers, and into our oceans.

You'd think, with microfibres being so tiny, that their impact on the environment would be too small to be noticeable. However, according to the United Nations Environment Programme, our laundry causes around half a million tonnes of plastic microfibres to be released into the ocean every year. **That's the equivalent of almost three billion polyester shirts!**

These microfibres can also act as mini sponges for chemicals in the water, meaning that a single microfibre can be up to **1,000 times more toxic** than the water around it! And, because they're so small, microfibres are often eaten by sea creatures. In fact, microfibres have even been gobbled up by plankton: tiny organisms that are too small to be seen with the naked eye! These plastics and the chemicals in them are then passed up the food chain when other animals eat the plankton, eventually reaching us.
HOW SCARY IS THAT?

Our Hero

Professor RICHARD THOMPSON

Richard Thompson OBE is a marine biologist who researches plastic pollution in the ocean. While doing beach cleans, he noticed that it was mostly the larger plastic objects that got all the attention. Richard's investigation into smaller plastics, which he called "microplastics", ended up shocking the world.

Why we think Richard is great...

Professor Richard Thompson has been a hero for us since we started Kids Against Plastic. He has been carrying out leading research into **microplastics** for many years, and still manages to relate the content he studies to ordinary people like us **(even when we were young children!)**. We've been incredibly grateful for his support and encouragement of **KIDS AGAINST PLASTIC**, particularly when it comes to our own research into microplastics and microfibres.

Dear Diary,

Our microfibre mission!

What happens to the **BILLIONS OF HARMFUL MICROFIBRES** that are generated by the population of a city, all using their washing machines every day? Surely the water companies are responsible for filtering this waste before it is returned to **our rivers and oceans?**

This was the question that Ella and I had once we'd found out first-hand that our own washing machine was generating **THOUSANDS OF MICROFIBRES** from the clothes we were washing. We discovered this by simply attaching a **MICROFILTER** to our washing machine's outlet pipe, and found that we were able to trap the tiny plastic fibres. Using a simple microscope lens that clipped onto our phone, we saw, with our own eyes, the shocking amount of fibres that were washing down our drain.

But what wasn't clear to us was **what happens to these fibres** once they are expelled from our washing machine. Could we be confident that our water treatment company would be trapping these fibres before they were able to reach our local river, the River Trent, and then on to the sea?

We needed to investigate...

So, armed with a DIY microfibre net, we headed to Stoke Bardolph to sample treated waste water from our home city, Nottingham. The water treatment plant sits literally a few hundred metres away from the river. Our net secured in place, we began sampling the treated **EFFLUENT**, or liquid waste, that was on its way into the river.

While we were aware that our sampling was quite basic and non-scientific, we didn't think it mattered. All we were trying to find out was if it is possible for any plastic microfibres to **pass through the water treatment process.**

After using a special filter and a better microscope in a university laboratory, we could say with some confidence that plastic microfibres are making their way into the rivers that feed our oceans. Sadly, we had the evidence that we were looking for.

BIOPLASTICS

BIOPLASTICS! This new type of plastic is relatively new on the materials scene, and has been getting a lot of attention.

Bioplastics are basically plastics that have been made from plant material, such as wood chippings or food waste, and are often sold as an **environmentally-friendly** version of plastics made from oil.

You'd think that, being made from natural stuff, bioplastics would be the perfect eco-friendly alternative to plastic. But unfortunately, there are quite a few issues when it comes to these plant plastics.

Now, if we were to list ALL the problems with bioplastics, we'd have a pretty thick book and a **sore head** from all the complicated science-y stuff. So, let's stick to the main problem with them...

... THEY'RE SUPER HARD TO DISPOSE OF!

So, do you put bioplastics in the recycling bin like some normal plastics?

Nope!

Well, do you put them in your garden waste?

Normally, this is a big no too, as there are so many different types of bioplastic and they all break down at different rates and in different conditions!

Well, what on earth are we meant to do with them? It sounds like there's no way of getting rid of bioplastics, and I don't want to keep them in my bedroom!

Well, most bioplastics just end up being put in the general waste bin like the majority of plastics anyway — which doesn't make them that much better than the material we're avoiding in the first place. UGH!

BREAKING it down

We often see bioplastics described as compostable or biodegradable. But just what is the difference? Let's try to clear up just what these terms mean.

Compostable

Does that word sound familiar? Compost is basically broken-down natural materials. Some people scatter it around their gardens to help their plants grow. You may have seen it before – it looks a lot like soil, but is much smellier! Well, a similar concept applies to compostable plastics, but instead of fruit and vegetables breaking down, it's plastic! For a plastic to be compostable, it needs to be able to break down in an industrial composter – a machine that is like a big version of household compost bins. Most compostable plastics won't break down quickly if just thrown outside. For composting to work, you need conditions to be warm, with plenty of moisture and oxygen.

I've been here since 1980!

Biodegradable

Unlike compostable plastic, biodegradable plastics don't need controlled conditions to break down. Most biodegradable materials are designed to break down in the environment, such as at a landfill site. However, it still takes around six months for biodegradable plastics to actually break down. They can also release greenhouse gases – the main gases that cause global warming – in the process! Also, if biodegradable plastics break down in the wrong conditions, they can fragment into smaller pieces. These framents pollute the landscape, and animals can eat them.

It's important to remember that just because a plastic is compostable or biodegradable, that doesn't mean it's okay to litter! These plastics can still last long enough to cause damage to wildlife and ecosystems.

Impact on WILDLIFE

It can sometimes be easy for humans to ignore the negative effects of our plastic habits. No-one likes to drive past hundreds of plastic bottles lying on the side of the road, or see a plastic bag tangled in a tree like some kind of ugly bunting. But, plastic is often thought of as being out of sight, out of mind. Unfortunately, this isn't the case for the wildlife we share the planet with!

Over 100,000 sea mammals are killed by plastic in the oceans every year...

... along with one million sea birds. Even mussels, the shellfish whose pretty blue shells you often find on the beach, are eating plastic — a study done on mussels in the UK found tiny pieces of plastic in all of them. **Yum!** But it's not just sea animals that are affected by plastic. Plastic that doesn't make its way into the oceans can be dreadful for land wildlife. Plastic packaging can easily get stuck around the head or neck of an animal, or even tangled around their legs. Many animals such as cows can also die from eating plastic bags and other items that blow into their fields.

MORE THAN 90% OF SEABIRDS ARE ESTIMATED TO HAVE PLASTIC IN THEIR GUTS!

Plastic is impacting animals big and small. If we're not careful, our rubbish could have a terrible long-term effect on wildlife.

When we go swimming in the sea, we might have to get used to seeing plastic instead of fish — now that's not the nicest sight while snorkelling!

A PLASTIC whale?

In 2017, the small Norwegian island of Sotra, near Bergen, became the setting for what is becoming an all-too familiar story. A dying whale got washed up on a beach, its stomach full of plastic, reinforcing the message that we need to do something about our plastic habits, and fast! **Why?** Well, this whale is just another example of how our use and abuse of throw-away plastic is damaging our ocean ecosystems and wildlife.

On this occasion, the unfortunate whale was a **Cuvier's beaked whale** – a species that is never typically seen so close to our shorelines. They normally live way out at sea, diving to depths of more than a mile in search of flavoursome deep-sea fish. This is how they've lived, happily, for millions of years. But, instead, this malnourished **"plastic whale"** came close to land and suffered a painful and early death.

The whale, like many before it, had mistaken plastic bags floating in the ocean for food. It had eaten so much of this plastic pollution that **30 PLASTIC BAGS** were removed from its stomach. With a tummy full of plastic, it probably didn't feel hungry, and the poor sea mammal unknowingly went without the nutrients and energy that it needed to survive. It ultimately starved itself to death.

SOMEWHERE IN THE REGION OF 8-12 MILLION METRIC TONNES OF PLASTIC POLLUTION ENTER THE WORLD'S OCEANS EVERY YEAR.

Unfortunately, desperately sad stories like this one will become more and more common. Until us humans ditch our addiction to convenience plastics and become more responsible. The alternative is *not good news* for these precious mammals.

Interview with...

MADDIE MOATE

Maddie Moate is an **EduTuber**. Now that's not a profession you hear about every day! Basically, she produces videos on YouTube that make learning about science more fun. Maddie has over **25 MILLION** views on her films across different channels, which include videos about plastic that she's presented for **BBC Earth Unplugged** and **Recycle Now**. How impressive is that?! Maddie is also a kids' TV presenter and won a **BAFTA** (British Academy of Film and Television Arts) for her work in 2017.

Q: HAVE YOU PERSONALLY SEEN THE IMPACT THAT PLASTIC IS HAVING ON OUR PLANET?

A: I can honestly say that in the past five years, or at least since the plastic problem has come to the forefront of my mind, I haven't seen a beach untouched by plastic pollution. It makes me extremely angry to see our wild environments being spoilt in this way. More recently I've stayed in seaside-resort accommodation where staff are employed to traipse up and down the "pristine" shoreline, continually collecting the rubbish and plastic as it washes up on the sand. While I'm all for a beach clean, I can't help but feel that hiding the scale of the issue from tourists somehow diminishes the problem. It's something we should all have to face.

Q: WHAT IS THE MOST SHOCKING THING YOU'VE LEARNED ABOUT SINGLE-USE PLASTIC WHILE YOU'VE BEEN MAKING VIDEOS FOR KIDS?

A: I am constantly in awe of the human feats of engineering I see in factories that I visit for filming. The machinery we have created to make mass manufacturing possible is spectacular, but all too often the last step in the process involves wrapping a product in plastic. There's something pretty terrifying about seeing first-hand over 1 million plastic bottles pass through a single factory floor in one day.

Q: AS A SUCCESSFUL PRESENTER, DO YOU HAVE ANY TIPS FOR YOUNG PEOPLE WHO WANT TO GET THEIR MESSAGE ACROSS TO OTHERS?

A: Just to be your authentic self and find original ways to talk about the things you really care about.

Q: ARE YOU OPTIMISTIC ABOUT THE FUTURE OF THE ENVIRONMENT?

A: I am optimistic. Everyone is finally talking about the changes they're making to improve the health of our planet. Slowly but surely, people are recognising the problem and stepping up. The biggest impact is coming from the younger generations though – they've decided they've had enough and that things need to change. Their voice is loud and powerful, which makes me extremely excited about our future leaders.

Our Hero

Sir DAVID ATTENBOROUGH

Sir David Attenborough is a famous natural historian and TV presenter. He is known for writing and presenting documentaries about animals and plants from all over the world. Many species have been named in his honour, including a carnivorous plant, a tropical butterfly, and one of the world's smallest frogs.

Why we think David is great...

If you asked most British environmentalists who their hero is, you would probably hear David Attenborough's name. We grew up watching his nature documentaries on TV, and they helped us to understand more about the natural world and why we should be taking care of it, eventually driving us to start **Kids Against Plastic**.

You need to connect with the world around you in order to be passionate about protecting it, and David's work shows us just how amazing and diverse the natural world is.

PLASTIC and us

We know that the wildlife we share the planet with are eating our plastic litter – but what about us?

Now, obviously we're not talking about people accidentally eating a plastic bag instead of a fish, like many sea creatures. But, what if plastic was making its way onto our plates in more unexpected ways?

This isn't what I ordered!

It's estimated that one human eats at least 50,000 pieces of microplastic every year!

These come from a range of different sources – be it the food we eat, the water we drink, and even the air we breathe.

It's been found that bottled water contains a high amount of these tiny plastic particles.

And almost all mussels contain plastic, so it's likely that we're eating the plastic that they've ingested too!

Microplastics have even been found in rainwater in remote mountain ranges.

YUCK, so I could be eating plastic every time I have a meal or take a drink?

Yes! Now, at the moment we don't know just what effect this is having on our bodies. But hopefully, as more research is done into microplastics, we'll find out more about the long-term impacts of eating plastic.

WHO'S to blame?

SO, WHO'S TO BLAME FOR THE PLASTIC POLLUTION CRISIS? Well, we all play a part in generating masses of plastic waste. But, let's take a look at some of the industries that are the big players when it comes to plastic pollution.

Drinks

Drinks companies are undoubtedly big contributors to the issue of plastic pollution. They produce billions of plastic bottles every year. Coca-Cola has been found to be the most polluting brand in both the 2018 and 2019 global waste audits (run by the **#breakfreefromplastic** movement), with Pepsi also ranking highly.

The other issue is that many drinks companies look to recycling as the plastic pollution solution – a flawed approach as the global plastic recycling rate lies at around the 18% mark.

Food

The global brands that produce packaged food are a big contributor to plastic pollution. Nestlé, the largest food company in the world, ranked very highly in the 2019 waste audit, producing on average more than one million tonnes of waste each year. Also, some crisp companies produce more than 11 million packets a day!

There is some action being taken, though. Walkers – one of the major crisp manufacturers in the UK – has started collecting crisp packets for recycling, after widespread campaigning for them to make their packaging more recyclable. This is great news, and it shows the power that we consumers can have!

Takeaways

Anyone who's been on a litter pick will be no stranger to finding fast food packaging! Not only are food containers often made of cheap polystyrene (PS), which is incredibly hard to recycle, but most fast food chains also include plastic toys in their meals. The good news is some large fast food companies have taken pledges to ban plastic straws or reduce the number of plastic toys given out, including Burger King and McDonald's.

SAY NO TO PLASTIC!

Now, instead of just pointing the finger at these companies, it's important to remember that being a part of a problem makes you a big part of the solution.

WE, AS THE PEOPLE WHO BUY THESE COMPANIES' PRODUCTS, HAVE A VOICE THROUGH OUR PURCHASES.

Let's make sure that we encourage those who generate the plastic waste to reduce it, but let's also make an effort to tackle this problem together.

AFTER ALL, WE'RE ALL RESPONSIBLE, SO WE ALL HAVE TO WORK TOWARDS THE SOLUTION!

Interview with...

WILL McCALLUM

Will is the **Head of Oceans at Greenpeace UK**, so he certainly knows his stuff when it comes to ocean pollution! Greenpeace has been responsible for many campaigns that put pressure on big corporations and governments to be more environmentally conscious, particularly when it comes to plastic usage. Will has also written a book called *How to Give Up Plastic*.

Q: WHAT IS GREENPEACE'S MESSAGE TO LARGE COMPANIES WHEN IT COMES TO SINGLE-USE PLASTIC?
A: Reduce, reduce, reduce. And if that means shifting your business model, then start planning now, because change is coming whether you like it or not. Companies have profited for too long by escaping responsibility for the products they put out into the world, and we have to see ambitious leaders step up now.

Companies need to set dramatic reduction targets for single-use plastic that look at eliminating packaging wherever possible. Companies that are serious about change also need to start educating other businesses, because collective action is the only way we're going to end this problem.

Q: HOW CAN WE, AS ORDINARY PEOPLE, HELP TO DRIVE COMPANIES TO CHANGE?

A: Never stop talking about it to the companies you come across. The only reason they will act is if they feel the pressure to, so even when you know you're being annoying, make sure to raise your voice. Ask them difficult questions, take pictures of packaging you don't think is necessary and post them online, write to customer service managers to complain, and more!

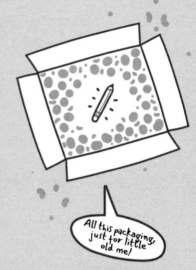

All this packaging, just for little old me!

Q: DO YOU THINK THE ACTIONS OF YOUNG ACTIVISTS CAN MAKE A DIFFERENCE?

A: The actions of young people have made all the difference. Without students from across the world raising their voices, we would not have anything like the amount of politicians and decision makers taking an interest in the environment. Young people need to keep on demanding a future they deserve.

Q: HAVE YOU ALWAYS BEEN INVOLVED IN ACTIVISM? WHAT INSPIRED YOU TO TACKLE ENVIRONMENTAL ISSUES?

A: I was always interested in nature and the environment, inspired by nature documentaries. But I got involved in activism a bit later – during university when friends and lecturers helped me to understand the need for activism for political action. I learnt about social movements in other parts of the world and could see that climate change was an issue that was going to need a huge social movement to overcome it. Nearly 15 years later I've participated in all kinds of activism, but I always come back to the environment – because for a better future, we need a healthy planet.

PLASTIC and CLIMATE CHANGE

It's easy to think that all the big environmental issues — **plastic pollution, air pollution, and climate change, to name a few** — are unrelated. After all, how can an increase in global temperature or rising sea levels relate to plastic? Well, there are actually a lot of links between our use of plastic and climate change, believe it or not!

CLIMATE CHANGE IS DEFINED AS A LONG-TERM SHIFT IN GLOBAL OR REGIONAL CLIMATE PATTERNS OVER A SIGNIFICANT PERIOD OF TIME.

Basically, climate change is a term that describes all of the changes in weather related to a rise in global temperature. Climate change is affected by lots of things, **particularly a gas called carbon dioxide**. Carbon dioxide (CO^2) occurs naturally in the atmosphere — however, many human activities release even more carbon dioxide into the atmosphere, which contributes to an increasing global temperature.

The trails left by planes help trap heat inside the atmosphere.

On average, one car emits 4.6 tonnes of CO_2 each year.

Power plants release lots of toxic gases into the atmosphere, including CO_2.

73

The Carbon CYCLE

Not all carbon dioxide comes from humans. In fact, carbon has an **amazing** natural cycle – **and it involves almost all life on Earth.**

Respiration

Both plants and animals use a process called respiration, by which they convert oxygen and sugar into energy for growth and movement. Carbon dioxide is a by-product of this that is released into the atmosphere. But don't worry, your body respiring isn't a main cause of global warming.

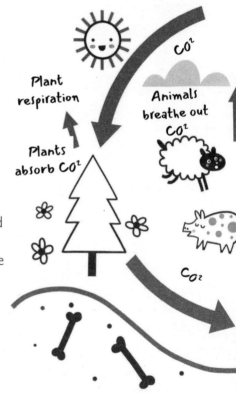

Plant respiration

CO_2

Animals breathe out CO_2

Plants absorb CO_2

CO_2

Dead organisms

When a plant or animal dies in the wild, it is broken down by very small microbes called decomposers. These release carbon dioxide through respiration too!

74

Photosynthesis

Plants produce food through a process called photosynthesis. In order to photosynthesise, plants need to absorb carbon dioxide from the atmosphere – which is why trees are so important in helping prevent climate change!

CO_2

Factories release CO_2

Animals die

CO_2

Fossilise

Over time, the remains of plants and animals can turn into fossil fuels, like oil or gas. When we burn these fuels, we release the huge amount of carbon stored in them into the atmosphere as carbon dioxide.

Plastic is responsible for a growing amount of carbon dioxide production. First of all, **fossil fuels** – resources that are made up of the remains of dead plants and animals from a long time ago, and are one of the leading causes of climate change – are required to make plastic!

On top of this, plastic contributes to carbon dioxide release throughout its lifetime, even after we've finished with it and thrown it away.

ESTIMATES SUGGEST THAT THE LIFE CYCLE OF THE WORLD'S PLASTICS – FROM BEING MADE TO AFTER BEING DISCARDED – WILL PRODUCE AS MUCH CARBON DIOXIDE PER YEAR AS 615 COAL POWER PLANTS WILL BY 2050!

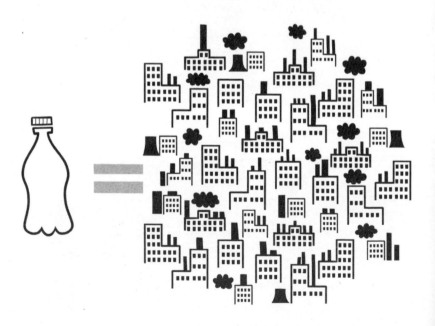

IT'S SCARY HOW ONE OF THE
MATERIALS WE USE EVERY DAY
IS HAVING SUCH AN IMPACT ON
THE CHANGING CLIMATE –
SOMETHING WHICH ENDANGERS
HUMAN LIFE ITSELF!

"The GREATEST THREAT to our planet is the belief that SOMEONE ELSE WILL SAVE IT."

Robert Swan

Robert Swan OBE is the first person to have walked to both the North and South poles. He has organised several cleanups removing and recycling rubbish left behind at Arctic and Antarctic stations. Robert is an advocate of renewable energy and has sailed around the world on a sailboat powered by wind, solar, and biodiesel energy.

Dear Diary,

An unstoppable tide of plastic

Arrochar is a little village in the Scottish Highlands that is positioned at the head of Loch Long. It's a picturesque place – a tourist hotspot for the area – but that wasn't what drew us there. Instead, it was the news that every day, a smelly and plastic-laden tide deposits its cargo onto the loch shore.

We decided to investigate...

What we discovered when we arrived at Arrochar was even worse than we expected. The unnaturally bright-coloured plastic items washed up on the beach could be seen all the way from the road. And sure enough, as we ventured down onto the beach, we stepped onto layer upon layer of **plastic-encrusted seaweed and mounds of plastic litter.** It was disgusting. It was also never going to stop because this rubbish was being brought into Arrochar twice daily as the tides came in. Arrochar wasn't the cause of this litter – it just happens to be in the **"PERFECT"** location – at the end of a flow of currents and waterways that bring waste from as far away as Australia and Japan.

Then, when we had a chat with a local B&B owner, we felt real sadness and despair. Not only is the plastic an awful sight for locals who have to see it every day, it's also not the best sight to see from the room of a B&B while on holiday in a beautiful spot in the Scottish Highlands! She was fighting an ongoing battle to clear up the incessant tide of plastic, but it was a fight that she was struggling to win.

WE JOINED IN WITH THE LOCAL MONTHLY BEACH CLEAN. ALTHOUGH WE SPENT SEVERAL HOURS WORKING, AND COLLECTED MANY BAGS OF RUBBISH, WE BARELY SCRATCHED AT THE SURFACE OF THIS BEACH'S PLASTIC PROBLEM.

The locals know that they are not the source of the plastic spoiling their beach, and that their efforts to clean it up are almost futile. But they are determined and will **never give up**. They keep raising awareness, and want to send a message to the powers that be to take the action that is desperately needed.

2

MAKE A CHANGE

So, you've found out some of the ways that plastic is affecting the environment. But what can you do to reduce its impact? We've all got to do our bit, be it big or small, so here are some ideas for ways to reduce your plastic usage at home and when you're out and about.

The Global GOALS

Back in 2015, leaders from around the world signed up to the **United Nations' Global Goals for Sustainable Development** (also known as the SDGs). Quite a mouthful, but these goals are super important – they are basically a call to action for all countries to work together to tackle big global issues that need addressing, urgently. They include ending poverty, ensuring zero hunger, and helping to preserve the environment for the future. Here are a couple of the goals that we think are really cool!

GOAL 12
Responsible consumption and production

Our planet has a lot of amazing resources – but we're using them too fast! If we're not careful, we're going to run out, so this goal is about making sure that we consume what we have on offer sustainably.

GOAL 14
Life below water

Oceans cover more than 70% of our planet. They are vital for our survival, but our actions are damaging them. Goal 14 aims to reduce pollution and overfishing in seas, and protect marine life.

In order to allow time to tackle these **BIIIG** issues, the goals have a 15-year timespan — with an end-date of 2030 (when the goals will be measured again and updated for another 15 years).

IN THE MEANTIME, IT'S IMPORTANT THAT WORLD LEADERS STEP UP THE PACE WHEN IT COMES TO GLOBAL ACTION - NOW!

But the United Nations stress that solving these problems can't just be done by the world leaders alone.

So, let's not leave it all up to the governments!
Let's look at some of the ways that you can get involved and make changes yourself to help address the issues included in the SDGs...

These goals are partly what inspired us to start Kids Against Plastic!

LITTER PICKING

We've done our fair share of litter picks in the past. They're a great way to have an immediate impact on the plastic pollution in your neighbourhood, as it doesn't take long to see a big difference.

However, it's important to **be careful** when picking up rubbish – sometimes there are items or places it is best to avoid. So, here are our top tips for staying safe while litter picking!

1 Think about your location

There are so many different places you can litter pick. Beaches, woodland paths, city streets... you can find rubbish almost anywhere that humans have been! However, often the places where you find the most litter are the ones that we use the most regularly, like near roads.

WE'VE DONE LITTER PICKS ON ROADSIDES AND COLLECTED MORE THAN 1,000 PIECES, JUST AS A FAMILY!

While you can achieve great results from litter picking along roadsides, they can also be **very dangerous**. Make sure you stay away from busy highways, and always stick to places with a pavement. Always have a parent or guardian with you, and ensure you wear something bright so you can be easily seen, such as a high-vis jacket.

Be hygienic

2

When litter picking, you often find items that aren't... particularly clean. Many times the rubbish has sat there for so long that it's covered in dirt and bacteria – **yuck!** That's why it's super important to stay safe and healthy when picking things up. Think about your gear – get hold of a litter picker and thick work gloves – you DON'T want to be using your bare hands.

ALWAYS MAKE SURE YOU HAVE A BOTTLE OF HAND SANITISER IN YOUR POCKET FOR WHEN YOU'RE DONE!

3

Be careful what you collect!

Just imagine, you've finished picking up for the day, you've got a full bag of rubbish that you're taking to the bin and – riiiip! Your bag has split, and dropped everything back onto the floor. This is a nightmare scenario that's happened to us many times! To avoid it happening, don't pick up anything sharp (like shattered glass, or needles). Not only are these items dangerous, they're also far more likely to rip your bag open than an item like a plastic bottle.

If something looks too gross (and trust me, you will find many strange things when litter picking), then just leave it. It's better to be safe than sorry!

TRY TO KEEP AN EYE OUT FOR ORGANISED LITTER PICKS IN YOUR AREA!
We've been on group litter picks before where we've collected over **2,000 pieces in just one hour** – such as one that we did on a beach in Cardiff, Wales. You can pick up incredible amounts when working together, and it also gives you a great sense of comradeship when working together to make a difference.

CLEANING it Up

It's surprising how much we can **learn from litter**. You'll find different types of rubbish depending on where you visit, and this can tell us a lot about where our waste comes from. If you record your litter picks, it can help to locate particular waste sources, for example you might find a sewer drain that washes out lots of wet wipes. There are some really easy ways to log the litter you pick up:

Marine Debris Tracker

The Marine Debris Tracker has, in its own words, been "tracking litter since before smartphones existed". It's no surprise that more than 2 million pieces of litter have been logged through this app in the years it's been running. It's super easy to use – all you need is a phone so you can download the app, then just use the categories to total up the litter you collect!

Be Plastic Clever

This is our own Kids Against Plastic app for logging litter! We worked with a mapping software company to create a map of litter around the world that you can add to yourself. Just head to our website and scan the QR code on our mapping page to access the survey and then you're good to go! Similarly to the Marine Debris Tracker, you log the litter in categories and then you can head to our website and see your collection appear as a dot on our map – cool, right?

kidsagainstplastic.co.uk/map

LOGGING YOUR LITTER IS A REALLY HELPFUL WAY OF FINDING OUT HOW OUR WASTE GETS INTO THE ENVIRONMENT - WHICH MEANS WE CAN STOP IT IN THE FIRST PLACE!

Citizen science – the collection of data about the planet that comes from members of the general public – is key to creating a map of our plastic waste. For example, if lots of cigarette butts are found in one area, action can be taken to encourage more responsible disposal of cigarettes there. These changes all come from the data that normal people, like us, collect!

"Us kids may only be 25% of the world's population, but we are 100% of the future."

Melati and Isabel Wijsen

Melati and Isabel Wijsen are two sisters who in 2013, aged 12 and 10, started a campaign called Bye Bye Plastic Bags on their native island of Bali, Indonesia. It has since become an international movement, and the Wijsens have spoken all over the world, and successfully lobbied the government to ban single-use plastics in Bali.

Dear Diary...

Sailing adventure (sort of!)

When we were asked by one of our inspirations, Emily Penn (who works tirelessly to protect our oceans) if we'd like to join her in a sailing project, we jumped at the chance. She wanted us to be the land-based **AMBASSADORS** for the *Round Britain* voyage she was running with her **eXXpedition** environmental organisation. OK, we'll be honest – it would have been even better if we got to be on their boat, *Sea Dragon* (cool name), but rules are rules and we were too young.

So, just to explain, the Round Britain voyage challenged an all-female crew to sail a 22 m (72 ft) boat around the British Isles, **sampling the seas for microplastics**. It was to take them 28 days in total, and not only would they collect samples to help advance research into ocean-based microplastics, they also planned to stop at ports along the way to engage with local people, including school kids, as well as the media and politicians.

THIS WAS WHERE KIDS AGAINST PLASTIC CAME IN! WE WOULD BE THEIR YOUTH REPRESENTATIVES.

At this stage, Kids Against Plastic had a **MOBILE EXHIBIT** that we used to demonstrate some of the issues around single-use plastic. It included lots of props like examples of plastics found on beaches and in ocean waters. We'd also show examples of non-plastic alternatives to encourage the use of reusable items, particularly for the **BIG 4** convenience plastic items...

CAN YOU REMEMBER THEM? YEP – CUPS AND LIDS, BOTTLES, STRAWS, AND BAGS.

During the trip, we got to speak to lots of young people and got a really positive vibe. This reinforced our thinking that **our generation is really concerned about the state of the environment**, and is very keen to do something about it.

We also got to meet some politicians and decision-makers, and spoke at the Scottish and Welsh Parliaments. But the highlight had to be when we were actually on the same discussion panel as **Professor Richard Thompson** – he's one of the leading academics in the field of ocean microplastics. You can read more about him on pages 48–49, as he's featured as one of our heroes!

The good news is that eXXpedition successfully completed their 28-day mission. The bad news is that they found microplastics in all of the areas they sampled... but I guess we all suspected — and dreaded — that that'd be the case.

Our
Hero

EMILY PENN

Emily Penn is an oceans advocate and skipper (boat captain). She is the co-founder of eXXpedition, a series of all-female voyages with the goal of investigating ocean plastic pollution. She was inspired to act after seeing the five ocean gyres in person, and finding out how many toxic chemicals end up in our bodies from microplastics.

Why we think Emily is great...

Emily helped inspire us to start Kids Against Plastic. She introduced us to the term 'gyre' (the ocean currents where plastic accumulates) when we first met her back in 2013 – at the time, we were around 10 and 8 years old – and we've been learning from her ever since!

It is so inspiring for us to see an empowered woman like Emily working with companies to reduce their plastic usage and leading research into the problem. Her work with eXXpedition also helped us understand so much more about the unseen impacts of plastic. We loved joining her during one of her eXXpedition trips as the land-based ambassadors.

Being Plastic CLEVER

"Plastic Clever" is an idea that we came up with as part of Kids Against Plastic to help people to do their bit to tackle plastic pollution.

We're so often told to become plastic-free, when actually, this is something that is impossible for most people —including us!

So, instead we came up with what we call "Plastic Clever". It's about being smarter with our use of plastic — and it starts with reducing our use of four items in particular...

The Worst
OFFENDERS

These four items are all in the top ten of objects polluting our oceans. We often use them just once, for a very short amount of time, before disposing of them.

Plastic cups and lids
Fewer than 1% of coffee cups are recycled.

Plastic bottles
Billions of plastic bottles are sold worldwide every year.

Plastic straws
Every year plastic straws injure millions of animals who mistake them for food.

Plastic bags
Most people use a plastic bag for just 15 minutes.

Often, you can use reusable items

Plastic-bottled water can cost more per litre than car fuel! Save yourself some money by investing in a **reusable bottle** that you can drink from time and time again. If the tap water in your area is unsafe to drink, look for a bottle with a filter in the lid. These make sure that you stay healthy while also reducing your plastic usage.

More and more coffee shops are offering discounts on your drink if you bring your own **reusable mug**. So, spending a bit more on a reusable item that you can use over and over not only helps to save the planet, it also puts a bit more cash in your pocket.

as a simple alternative to plastic.

Plastic bags can be replaced with **tote** ones for shopping. Most supermarkets now sell these! When it comes to loose fruit and vegetables, it's worth encouraging your parents or carers to get hold of some reusable **mesh bags**, instead of the single-use bags provided.

And finally, plastic straws! You often find straws put in your drink automatically, so make sure to say **"no straw, please!"** as part of your order. If you still want a straw for your drink, there are many non-plastic reusable alternatives on sale – including metal, silicon, and bamboo.

Following these steps is much simpler than going completely plastic-free, and yet can still have a big positive impact. We cannot underestimate the power we have if we all take simple actions to reduce our use of plastic. After all, it's our collective habits that have fuelled the plastic pollution crisis in the first place, so it's up to us to fix it.

Be More Eco-friendly
AT HOME

So, you've got some tips on how to be more Plastic Clever when out and about, but what about at home? Our houses are the perfect place to start making changes to reduce our environmental impact. Here are a few tips to get you started!

Make your food storage more Plastic Clever

Clingfilm is one of the worst forms of single-use plastic. It's really thin and is easily contaminated by food, meaning it often can't be recycled or used more than once. So, try to avoid covering or wrapping food with plastic wrap, and instead use a foil or reusable rubber alternative. Think about what's going in your lunch box! Also try to stay away from items that are packaged in unnecessary plastic – many on-the-go lunches are incredibly wasteful!

Reduce your microfibre output

When washing and drying your clothes, **be aware of your plastic microfibre output**. There are products that help to catch microfibres from your clothes during a wash – such as the Cora Ball or Guppy Bag – so that the microfibres don't get into the environment.

However, the best thing to do is to try to prevent microfibres in the first place. So **BUY CLOTHES THAT ARE MADE FROM NATURAL MATERIALS** like cotton or linen. Fibres from these materials biodegrade, or break down, if they enter the environment. Steer clear of clothes made from polyester and acrylic when possible. It's also been proven that washing your clothes on "delicate" washes causes more microfibres to shed (they use more water, which plucks the microscopic fibres from our clothes), so try to avoid this setting as much as possible.

Be aware of your energy consumption

We are often told to turn off our lights when we leave rooms. There's more to this than you might think, though. Around **80% of global energy is non-renewable,** meaning it comes from fossil fuels. When burned, many of these fuels produce carbon dioxide, which contributes to climate change. So, by reducing the amount of overall energy you use at home, you'll be minimising your impact on global warming. And saving the bill payers money on wasted electricity!

Swapping your **LIGHTBULBS** is a good way to reduce the amount of energy you use at home. LED lightbulbs use up to 80% less energy than traditional bulbs – that's a crazy amount!

The amount of carbon dioxide we release day-to-day is known as our "carbon footprint".

Hang your clothes up to dry when possible, instead of putting them in a dryer. **Clothes dryers** are the third most energy-consuming appliance in the house. Just think, by hang-drying your clothes two or three times a week, instead of putting them in the dryer, how much of an impact you could have!

CELEBRATIONS

Whenever you think about parties, the chances are that sparkly decorations or shiny wrapping paper are some of the first things to come into your head. Unfortunately, **a lot of these things are made of plastic.** Now, we are not here to be party-poopers and ruin your fun, but instead to give you some ideas on how you can make your celebrations something to really... well, **CELEBRATE!**

Get in the kitchen!

Let's be honest – there's nothing better than some nice home cooking. Plus, it's a perfect way to eliminate some of your plastic usage at home! A lot of celebration foods come wrapped in a huge amount of plastic packing that can be pretty easily avoided. Try making your own gingerbread for the Christmas table, doughnuts for Hanukkah, and rice pudding for Diwali. And, if you really want to impress guests with your skills, make and decorate your own Easter eggs using melted chocolate and a mould!

Wrapping Paper

Ever heard of the scrunch test? This little trick is the way to tell whether your wrapping paper is recyclable or not, and it's as easy as it sounds. If you scrunch up your wrapping paper and it stays in a tight ball, the chances are it's made of a natural material like paper and can be recycled. If not, it's probably partly made up of foil or plastic, meaning it has to go in your general waste. Try to avoid buying shiny or glittery wrapping paper – this is a good indicator that the material is probably plastic.

BROWN PAPER OR NEWSPAPER ARE GOOD SUBSTITUTES FOR WRAPPING PAPER.

In the UK, at Christmas, we use an average of **FOUR ROLLS** of wrapping paper per household – *that's an insane amount!* So, if you want to ditch the wrapping paper altogether, wrapping your presents in pretty cloths, scarves, and ribbons that can be used again is a lovely alternative. It also adds a special personal touch to the gift!

Balloons

Balloons are the iconic decoration when it comes to celebrations like birthdays, but it might be about time we rethink our use of them! When released into the environment, balloons can cause the deaths of wild animals that eat them or get tangled up in their tassels. This means that balloon releases are really something to avoid, and that balloons in general are not something that we should entertain.

Some balloons use up helium, a natural gas that we're running out of in our atmosphere, and become non-recyclable waste as soon as the occasion is over. Like with many single-use items, we've just got to think... do we really need them?

Paper decorations

Fancy getting your fingers a bit sticky? Paper chains make simple but effective decorations for any celebration, and all they require is some patience (and some pretty paper and glue, of course)! Diwali is an amazing example of how lovely paper decorations can be. Many Diwali and Lunar New Year decorations are made from paper **AND THEY LOOK BEAUTIFUL!** Try making your own paper chains for Christmas, or paper bunting and banners for Hanukkah or Eid to avoid plastic shop-bought decorations.

Make paper snowflakes

1 Take a square piece of paper and fold it in half diagonally.

2 Fold this shape in half again to create a smaller triangle.

3 Then fold the front and back thirds into the middle.

4 Using safety scissors, cut off the points at the bottom.

5 Now snip away, then unfold the flake.

SEE WHAT SHAPES UNFOLD!

The NON-PLASTIC
alternatives

So, we know that single-use plastics are bad for the planet. This means that the solution is to just get rid of them all together, and replace them with alternative materials, right?

Not quite. While we need to reduce the amount of plastic we use, we also need to think about the impact that alternatives to plastic have. After all, we don't want the same problem arising, but just with glass bottles instead of plastic!

Let's take a look at the positives and negatives of some plastic-free packaging alternatives!

Aluminium

Aluminium cans are much lighter than glass or plastic bottles. They also don't lose quality when they're recycled, so they can be recycled an infinite amount of times. For plastic, this number is in the single figures. However, aluminium is a metal. This means that if we don't properly recycle our cans, we need to mine more aluminium to make new ones. If we're not careful, we're going to run out of aluminium.

Glass

Normally, glass is looked at as the best material to use instead of plastic. After all, we used to use it for milk and other soft drinks before plastic became so popular. Unlike plastic, it doesn't have the same health risks associated with chemicals leaching into liquids. But, if you pick up a glass and a plastic bottle, it's not hard to notice one of glass's key flaws – it's super heavy! In fact, glass bottles are on average 40 times heavier than a plastic bottle. While this can be a bit annoying for us when we drink from glass, it's even worse when it comes to transporting it. It means more fuel is needed to transport glass, which leads to more carbon dioxide (CO_2) emissions. CO_2 is one of the key gases that causes climate change. So, maybe glass isn't so great after all!

Cartons

Cartons are often used as a substitute for plastic bottles. They're light and durable due to their layered structure of paper, metal, and plastic. However, this structure is one of the key issues with cartons – it makes them very hard to recycle! Can you imagine how complicated it is to have to separate all those different materials? It's no wonder that cartons often can't be completely recycled.

However, this is starting to change. Many recycling facilities are developing ways of dealing with cartons. Make sure to check your local recycling facilities to see if they accept them.

Ultimately, the best thing we can do is to try to reduce the amount of packaging we use altogether.

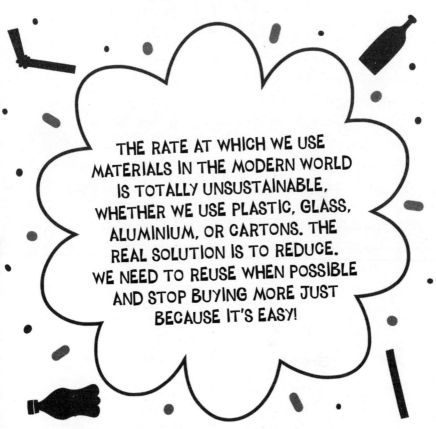

THE RATE AT WHICH WE USE MATERIALS IN THE MODERN WORLD IS TOTALLY UNSUSTAINABLE, WHETHER WE USE PLASTIC, GLASS, ALUMINIUM, OR CARTONS. THE REAL SOLUTION IS TO REDUCE. WE NEED TO REUSE WHEN POSSIBLE AND STOP BUYING MORE JUST BECAUSE IT'S EASY!

It's also up to brands to invest in looking for more sustainable materials, and to reduce the amount of packaging they use. **When buying products, try to look for brands that are environmentally conscious** – the best way to promote more sustainable practices in companies is to reward those that are taking positive steps already!

Being Plastic Clever
AT SCHOOL

Once you've taken steps to reduce your use of plastic at home, why not help your school to become **Plastic Clever**? As part of Kids Against Plastic, we've put together loads of resources and a step-by-step Plastic Clever guide for schools – just head to our website to sign up!

kidsagainstplastic.co.uk/do/plasticcleverschools

It might be a bit tricky to get your school and friends on board to begin with, so here are some ways that you can get them involved!

Start a club

If your school has an eco club, this is the perfect way to start launching Plastic Clever, as that way you have other students helping you! Make sure that you talk about plastic pollution and the problems it causes at your meetings, and then try to find one plastic item used at your school to tackle first. This could be plastic bottles or plastic cutlery used for school meals. Then, take steps to reduce your school's use of these items by speaking to your teachers and using our Plastic Clever resources. Working with a club of eco-minded people means that you're not in it alone!

Speak to your headteacher

Your headteacher has a lot of control over what happens at school, so try to involve them. You could write a letter or arrange to meet with them. This can be a bit scary, but remember that your teachers are there to support you and your learning. If plastic pollution is something that you're passionate about, most teachers (including headteachers) will often be more than keen to support you.

Give an assembly

Want to get your whole school on board? An assembly is the perfect way to do this. Even if you only speak for a minute or two, or do it with a group of friends (or eco club!), it's the perfect way to reach lots of your fellow students and get them involved with what you're doing.

You can find more tips and tricks about overcoming your nerves and giving a talk in the next chapter.

3

BEING AN
ACTIVIST

The small actions that we take can really make
a big difference in the long run – every little bit
counts, if we all work together. But what if you
wanted to do more, and take a bigger stand
for what you believe in? This next chapter is all
about how you can be an activist yourself, and
take action for an issue you're passionate
about – be it plastic-related or not!

How
KIDS AGAINST
PLASTIC began...

We were first inspired to start **Kids Against Plastic** in 2016, after studying the UN's Global Goals for Sustainable Development – as mentioned earlier in the book. At the time, we were being homeschooled by our parents and, being children who have always cared for the environment and the world we live in, they thought it was a fitting topic for us to study.

Through the Global Goals we discovered more about plastic pollution and the devastating impact that our single-use plastic habits are having on the environment. We were shocked by all of the horrible images of animals entangled in plastic, and the huge number of single-use plastic items we use globally every year. But what surprised us even more was that so few people – including ourselves – knew about this problem!

TO US, THIS SEEMED CRAZY, AND SOMETHING THAT WE NEEDED TO TAKE ACTION AGAINST AND CHANGE. AND SO, KIDS AGAINST PLASTIC WAS BORN.

Now, years later, **Kids Against Plastic** is a registered charity that has expanded around the UK and abroad. Here are some of the things we get up to:

Be Plastic Clever

We mentioned earlier in the book the idea of being 'Plastic Clever' – prioritising reusable items over single-use plastics. Now, **Plastic Clever** is something that we should all try to be, but our campaign also works with schools, businesses, cafes and more to help them become Plastic Clever, too!

We made resources for schools to include in their lessons, and are working with companies to help grow the Plastic Clever businesses scheme.

Basically, anywhere where there is an unnecessary use of single-use plastics can become Plastic Clever through the resources we made!

Picking up 100,000 pieces of litter

Yep, we're collecting **100,000 PIECES** of plastic litter — one for every sea mammal killed by plastic in the oceans every year! This was one of the first things we started doing when we founded Kids Against Plastic. It's taken a few years, but we're almost three quarters of the way to our goal — yay!

Youth empowerment

The most important thing that we do at Kids Against Plastic is encouraging other young people to have the belief that they can make a difference — just like we do! We think that us kids can have a really powerful voice, one that we often underestimate but that can be very influential. That's why one of the key focuses of Kids Against Plastic is schools — we do talks and make videos for schools to encourage more young people into activism. Hopefully it will inspire them to take action for what they believe in, too.

"The most dangerous phrase in the language is 'we've always done it this way'."

Grace Hopper

Grace Hopper (1906–1992) was a brilliant computer coding pioneer, and retired as the oldest serving officer in the U.S. Armed Forces. She joined the U.S. Naval Reserve during World War II, working as one of the first computer programmers. After the war, Grace led a team that created the first English-based computer language.

HAVE YOU BEEN INSPIRED TO TAKE ACTION AGAINST PLASTIC BY THIS BOOK – OR ARE YOU DOING SO ALREADY?

We would love to have you as part of our Kids Against Plastic team. We have more than 40 young people involved and taking action against plastic already! Make sure you get in touch and let us know what you're up to! Just go to:

kidsagainstplastic.co.uk/do/join

Starting a
CAMPAIGN

It's super inspiring to hear what other young people have done to make a difference, and hopefully you feel like you can do the same. But it can be a bit daunting – how on earth do I run a campaign, and start to take action? It's often said that first steps are the hardest ones to take, and it's no different for campaigning. So, here are some simple tips to help you get started.

1 Find your passion...

... and learn more about it! If you're keen to address plastic pollution, like us, then **fingers crossed** this book has helped you with this step. Campaigning takes commitment, so it's important that you're passionate about the issue you're tackling and willing to commit to it for a decent amount of time. Take a look at the UN's Sustainable Development Goals for inspiration, or see what other young activists have been up to around the world to find topics that might interest you.

2 Find a goal

The next step, when you've found the issue you'd like to tackle, is narrowing your focus. For example, for an issue like plastic pollution, it's impossible to just say "I want to stop all plastic pollution globally". This is way too big for anyone to achieve on their own! Give yourself a realistic goal to aim for – it can still be ambitious, but it should be achievable in the long run. Then, you can start taking small steps towards it.

The most important thing is not necessarily what you do, but just that you **do something**. No matter how big the issue, always remember you can make a difference. If everyone did their small bit then huge changes could take place!

When we first started Kids Against Plastic, we set ourselves the goal of picking up 100,000 pieces of plastic litter. This is a massive number, but it gave us something to aim for. And it was something that we knew that we could do, over time. We just had to take small steps towards it, by doing little litter picks regularly.

3 Raise awareness

We can't take on these global issues alone. It's really important to get others involved – spread the word! Tell your family, friends and classmates about what you're doing and why. Help them realise what they can do to help your campaign. This could be through doing an assembly at your school, or just doing something as simple as putting up posters.

The thing to remember about campaigning is that it isn't easy, but it's **definitely worth it**. Even if you just do something small in your local area, it can make a positive difference to where you live and the other people who live there.

RYAN HICKMAN

Ryan lives in the USA, and started his own recycling company when he was only **THREE YEARS OLD!** He collects recyclable items from people in his area, and takes them to the recycling centre. In return, he gets money, which he is saving to pay for his future university education. **Talk about forward thinking!** Ryan also makes and sells T-shirts to raise money for the Pacific Marine Mammal Center, which rescues and takes care of sea animals before releasing them back into the ocean. He is also a Youth Ambassador for the organisation. It's no wonder that Ryan's story has been featured around the world – in 2019 he was named by MSN as one of the top 15 kids changing the world!

Q: YOU WERE SO YOUNG WHEN YOU STARTED YOUR BUSINESS! WHAT INSPIRED YOU TO DO THIS AT SUCH A YOUNG AGE?

A: My dad took me to the recycling center for the first time when I was three and I just loved it, and I wanted to keep doing it.

Q: WHAT IMPACT HAVE YOU HAD THROUGH RYAN'S RECYCLING?

A: I've recycled over 750,000 plastic bottles and cans, so that's a lot not going into the oceans and landfill. I make videos and give speeches all the time about the importance of recycling and keeping our planet clean. I think I've made a lot of people think about recycling because I make it look pretty easy to them.

Q: WHY IS IT IMPORTANT TO RECYCLE?

A: It's important because when all of the recyclable items just go into the environment, animals suffer and it pollutes the oceans, rivers, and lakes. Most items take a long time to break down in the environment, so that's why it's so important to recycle.

Q: ANY ADVICE FOR OTHER KIDS ON HOW TO MAKE A DIFFERENCE? DO YOU THINK THAT AGE SHOULD BE A FACTOR WHEN IT COMES TO TAKING ACTION?

A: I always tell people that if a ten-year-old kid like me can follow my passion to make the world a better place, anyone else can too. You're never too young to make a difference. I know a lot of kids my age or even younger who are trying to do their part in saving the planet and taking care of the environment. Even small acts like picking up a piece of trash on the ground when you see it makes a difference. You might be saving an animal's life, and it cleans up the area too. :)

Interview with...

ELLA

Ella (another Ella!) is a member of our Kids Against Plastic team in the UK. She got involved tackling single-use plastic when she was only **SIX** years old! Together with her mum, she runs **Plastic Clever Salcombe**, where she visits local cafés and businesses and encourages them to **Be Plastic Clever**. She's also encouraged her school to do the same. Ella's done lots of litter picks, including on her local river using a stand-up paddleboard! So cool!

Q: WHAT ARE YOU DOING TO MAKE AN IMPACT ON PLASTIC IN YOUR LOCAL AREA?

A: I enjoy paddleboarding and while on the water, I collect rubbish as I go along. I do this regularly in Salcombe Estuary in Devon with my mum. We find so much rope, net, lots of plastic toys, bottles and bags, straws, crisp packets, and lots of other single-use litter.

Q: WHY DO YOU THINK IT'S IMPORTANT TO TACKLE PLASTIC POLLUTION?

A: It's important to tackle plastic pollution because if we don't reduce it soon, animals who get entangled or swallow any of the rubbish are at risk of becoming endangered. Plastic rubbish breaks up into microplastics which are around for hundreds of years.

Q: WHAT WOULD YOU SAY TO OTHER YOUNG PEOPLE WHO WANT TO DO SOMETHING FOR THE PLANET, BUT AREN'T SURE HOW TO GET STARTED?
A: It doesn't matter if you don't do one big thing. Little things can make a big difference, and you just have to believe in yourself!

Interview with...

LUCIE

Lucie is a member of the Kids Against Plastic team. She got really upset by the horrible impact that plastic is having on animals, and was inspired to do her bit against plastic pollution. Since then, she has been doing litter picks around her village and nearby beaches, and has put up posters encouraging people to collect litter. She does lots of work with her school to encourage them to **Be Plastic Clever**, and surveyed other pupils to see what their attitude is towards plastic pollution!

On top of all this amazing work, Lucie has also spoken about plastic at the European Union of Aquarium Curators, encouraging more aquariums to make a plastic pledge and reduce their use of plastic! How amazing is that?

Q: WHAT DO YOU AIM TO ACHIEVE THROUGH YOUR PLASTIC CAMPAIGNING?

A: I want to make everyone see exactly what we are doing to the planet. Lots of people are still not aware of the harm that plastic does, and some people only care because litter looks messy. I am still learning how harmful it can be, and the dangers that it can bring to our ecosystems. I would like to get rid of single-use plastic completely, and all of the plastics that are non-recyclable. We have the technology to stop using it but for some reason businesses and governments are not banning plastic. I don't know why, when to me it seems a simple and quick solution to a much bigger problem.

Q: WHY IS IT IMPORTANT FOR US TO MAKE A DIFFERENCE AS YOUNG PEOPLE?

A: It's important for us to show that if we can do it as young people, then so can adults. It is also important that young people start good habits now. In 30 years, we will be the ones in charge, and we will have no excuse to not make the right decisions. I don't know why we can't start now and why we have to wait for older people, it's our world too!

Q: WHAT CAN EVERYONE DO TO HELP TACKLE PLASTIC POLLUTION?

A: I would stay, start with something that you have the power to do. I am very lucky as my mum and dad support me and we tackle it together. However, I have friends who want to do things, but their parents don't want to help. So, they pick litter at school, or just refuse stuff made of plastic, or they recycle as much as they can. If you don't have much support, my advice would be to draw posters to put up in your school or local area, write letters or emails to companies that you know use single-use plastics, write to your local councillors, and ask your school to start a green club. If you are part of a club outside of school, such as Scouts or Girl Guiding, ask them if they would like to help, and put together a presentation to raise awareness about plastic pollution.

Interview with...

DANILO and SISLEY

Danilo Manuputty and his sister Sisley started their campaign **KICK (KEEP IT CLEAN KIDS)** in the Netherlands after discovering the harm that plastic waste is doing to the planet. They spread the word about being responsible with waste and not dropping litter, and are encouraging more young people to get involved in environmental action by speaking at schools, universities, and festivals. They've spoken at A Greener Festival in the UK, in Montenegro, and even on the Moluccan Islands in Indonesia!

Q: WHAT INSPIRED YOU TO START KICK?
DANILO: I was inspired to start KICK while visiting my family in Suli, a village on the Moluccan Islands in Indonesia. I was on the beach with my sister, in our kampong (village), and was shocked to see a lot of

waste and plastic in the sea. I immediately called my mother and asked her to explain this issue, and from that moment we, as a family, felt responsible to give something back to Mother Earth. So, KICK was born.

Q: WHAT DO YOU AIM TO ACHIEVE THROUGH WHAT YOU DO?
DANILO: I want a better world for the future so that everyone can live safely and cleanly.

Q: WHAT MESSAGE WOULD YOU GIVE TO YOUNG PEOPLE READING THIS?
DANILO: Just throw your trash in the trashbin and try to keep the beaches and everywhere you go tidy — let's make it a clean world!

Interview with...

DANIEL WEBB

Daniel Webb started a project called **EVERYDAY PLASTIC** back in 2017, where he collected all of his plastic waste for a **WHOLE YEAR!** What he found out was pretty scary – overall, he collected 4,490 pieces of plastic, which he calculated would mean that the whole UK population throws away **293 billion plastic items every year**. Of the plastic items he collected, **93%** were single-use plastic, **60%** were food packaging, and only **10%** would have been collected for recycling. Now, through Everyday Plastic, Dan aims to raise awareness of plastic usage, and help people realise the small, easy ways they can use less plastic in their everyday lives.

Q: WHAT INSPIRED YOU TO START EVERYDAY PLASTIC?
A: In 2016, I moved to the coastal town of Margate, Kent. Because of the swathes of plastic I was seeing washed up on the beach, I'd become more conscious of the massive amounts of packaging I was presented with in the supermarket. Twinned with the fact that I wasn't offered any recycling at my new home, there seemed to be no way to dispose of my plastic responsibly. So, I decided to conduct a little experiment... and store all of the plastic waste I generated for a year.

Q: WHAT SHOCKED YOU THE MOST WHEN COLLECTING ALL OF YOUR PLASTIC FOR A YEAR?

A: Seeing every piece of plastic that I threw away in a year all laid out in front of me, filling the floor space of a 2,000-capacity music venue, was one of the most surreal experiences I've ever had. The sad thing was that I barely remembered using any of the 4,490 items.

Q: WHAT CAN WE LEARN FROM COLLECTING OUR RUBBISH?

A: First, it provides us with a very personal connection to the problem. It shows us that the magnitude of global plastic pollution can be scaled right down to the individual. Most importantly, by seeing what we threw away the most, it helps us to identify where we can make simple lifestyle changes to help the planet.

Q: WHAT TIPS WOULD YOU GIVE YOUNG PEOPLE ON HOW TO BE MORE CONSCIOUS WITH OUR EVERYDAY USE OF PLASTIC?

A: Finding your own way to understand the plastic problem is really important. It's a very complex issue with many layers. Perhaps you want to help clean beaches, or encourage the supermarket to use less packaging. Maybe you just want to stop the school dishing out plastic cutlery. No matter how big or small, whatever you do really does make a difference.

Dear Diary...

Speaking to businesses

If, when we first started Kids Against Plastic, you'd have told us that a few years later we'd be speaking to one of the leading bottled water companies, we probably would have laughed. After all, it sounds like a pretty strange thing for anti-disposable plastic campaigners to do!

But that's exactly what we did. In **OCTOBER 2018**, we first stepped out in front of an audience of business people at a Danone Waters marketing conference. We spoke to them about the youth view on the plastic crisis, and how they needed to be doing more about the growing amount of plastic polluting our planet. It may seem like wouldn't have much to say to a company that is involved in causing the problem we've been tackling. However, Danone aren't the binary opposites to our charity that they may seem to be. In reality, it was uplifting for us to see what they are doing to take responsibility for the crisis they are contributing to. Danone have put work into not only meeting the **Plastics Pact** (a network of initiatives encouraging the involvement of businesses in reducing plastic waste), but also beating the recycled content targets. And, with two of Danone's brands at the time working towards 100% recycled PET bottles, it was clear to see it was an issue they were taking seriously.

We must not have done too bad of a job, as in July 2019 we then got invited back to speak at their Water the Future conference in Berlin. It was surreal to be invited to such an incredible city to speak at the conference – straight after Danone's CEO, Emmanuel Faber, no less!

We've been lucky enough to speak to numerous other businesses, too. In late 2019, we had the opportunity to visit Athens and speak at the American Hellenic Chamber of Commerce annual Corporate Responsibility conference (a bit of a mouthful!). At this conference, speakers discuss the impact that social and technological developments might have on businesses. We joined young activists from **Fridays for Future Athens**, part of the global school strike for climate change movement, on the closing panel of the event. It was brilliant to see a spotlight being put on the youth voice when it comes to the environmental issues that will ultimately be determining our futures.

We also got to speak to a completely different type of industry in Geneva – the airline industry! Not only was it good to speak to industry leaders about what they could be doing to reduce plastic waste and their carbon footprint, it was also a real eye opener for us on the issues that come with moving away from plastic. The airline industry is one in which plastic's key properties – being lightweight, durable, and cheap – are very useful, so it's difficult to stop using it completely. But, it's good to see action being taken despite this.

It just shows — in the field of activism, you have to be able to talk to everyone!

Our Hero

GRETA THUNBERG

Greta Thunberg (born 2003) is an environmental activist. After learning about climate change at the age of eight, she persuaded her family to cut down their carbon footprint. In August 2018, she started a school strike, demanding the Swedish government take stronger action against climate change. This sparked a school strike for climate change movement, with millions of young people across the world taking part.

Why we think Greta is great...

Greta has managed to do something that is very difficult – **get the world talking about environmental issues!** She is a role model for young people worldwide, and her work shows just how much of an impact kids can have. Greta has spoken openly about having Asperger Syndrome and its difficulties, but she also emphasises how being different can be good. She has travelled the world giving speeches to world parliaments, and joined other young activists in climate protests.

YOUTH STRIKE!

2019 was a significant year for several reasons – as well as being the last year of the decade, it was the year that marked the growth of a movement to tackle climate change, inspired largely by Greta Thunberg.

CLIMATE EMERGENCY

The Oxford Dictionary's 2019 word of the year was **"climate emergency"**. Not only does this demonstrate how climate issues are coming under the spotlight, it also shows the progression of attitudes. "Climate change" is no longer an acceptable way to describe this huge environmental threat to our planet. 2019 was the year that it was deemed the **climate crisis**, and the need for urgency on this issue was finally acknowledged.

FRIDAY ACTION

Greta Thunberg's school strike for climate change went viral on social media, and led to the creation of the global

Fridays for Future movement. Millions of young people began to step out of school every Friday to voice their concerns on the lack of climate action being taken. Local groups were formed to organise the strikes, and the movement gained the support of other environmental movements. A global climate strike was held on 15 March 2019.

STRIKE!

However, the biggest climate strike was the Earth Strike on **20 September 2019**. It was global, youth-led, and what's believed to be the largest climate protest in history. It is estimated that roughly **4 MILLION PEOPLE** took to the streets on the day, with gatherings happening in over **150 countries** around the world. Each protest often had its own focus, be it air pollution, plastic waste, or rising sea levels, but the message was universal and unanimous. We need to see urgent action for the climate, and we need to see it now.

While the Earth Strike was the largest in history, it will no

doubt soon be superseded. As concern grows, we will likely see larger and more powerful protests taking place, hopefully coupled with urgent climate action being taken by companies and governments.

THE START OF THE NEW DECADE IS FULL OF HOPE – HOPE THAT DESPITE THE DEVASTATING ISSUES FACING THE FUTURE OF THE PLANET, WE CAN COME TOGETHER AND MAKE A DIFFERENCE.

SPEAK UP!

Whether you're a kid or an adult, **PUBLIC SPEAKING** is a scary thing to do! There's something really daunting about putting yourself out there to talk in front of an audience, especially when it consists of your classmates. But, like anything, the more practise you get, the easier it becomes! We've been public speaking for a few years now, and we've put together some of our **TOP TIPS** on how to overcome the nerves (we all get them!) and own the stage.

1 Writing and planning

The key to doing a good speech is knowing what to say – and how to say it well! Speaking effectively is all about getting the right balance between **the facts and the funny**. If your talk is just a long list of facts, people will switch off (wouldn't you?!). But, if you focus too much on making it funny or comical, it can be hard to be taken seriously.

I'm so bored that I'm sleeping with my eyes open.

Also, consider your **AUDIENCE**. You wouldn't speak to your friends the same way you'd speak to an adult or teacher. Think about what's best to include – for example, there's no point talking about *how* to stop using plastic if people don't know *why* they should stop it to begin with!

When familiarising yourself with the script, try reading it out loud. This helps you to start learning the lines while getting to grips with pronunciation. It's a good idea to ask a family member or friend to listen to you read through your talk and give you pointers.

YOU COULD ALSO TRY USING AN APP TO RECORD YOURSELF SPEAKING. YOU MIGHT BE SURPRISED TO HEAR HOW DIFFERENT THE RECORDING SOUNDS TO HOW IT IS IN YOUR HEAD! DOING YOUR SPEECH IN FRONT OF A MIRROR CAN ALSO HELP YOU PRACTISE BODY LANGUAGE AND GESTURES.

2 Before the talk

Prepare, prepare, prepare. If you're feeling nervous, write out some **CUE CARDS**. Think about taking along some props to engage your audience while you speak. It can be as simple as bringing a reusable mug from home to hand around when you're encouraging people to use reusable items. **PROPS** really help to illustrate your point and keep your audience interested.

Only include key points on cue cards. Try not to read from them word-for-word — they're just there to jog your memory.

DON'T LET THE NERVES GET TO YOU!

If you look and act relaxed, even if you feel nervous inside, it will make others think that you're calm and know what you're doing. This leads to a better first impression. And, as odd as this may seem, clench your bum! No, we're not joking – doing this sends the blood from your legs to your core body and brain, helping you to concentrate and not feel faint. **Taking deep breaths** also helps, and thinking about your breathing can take your mind off any nerves.

TONGUE TIED
Voice warm up exercises

It's the stuff of nightmares to stand up to speak, only for your voice
to come out all croaky, or to have to stop to cough. But, thankfully,
it's an easy challenge to overcome. The solution is doing warm-ups!
You need to warm up your voice in the same way you'd warm up your
leg muscles before running. By doing this, you improve the sound of
your speech by making your tone flow more naturally, as well as by
preventing yourself from harming your voice. Here are a few fun ways
to warm up before your big moment:

Tongue twisters: Have a go at saying these, fast!

• The glowing groom in the growing gloom
• Irish wristwatch, Welsh wristwatch
• Similar cinema

Wait. Am I Irish or Welsh?

Mouth stretches: It might be better to find an empty or quiet
room for these! Try making these noises:

• "ahhhh" (like a long "r")
• "eeeee"
• "ceeee" (like "sea")
• "wawawa" (like an ambulance!)

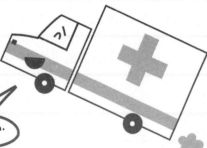

I'm ready to give my screech.
I mean speech!

147

3 Speaking speed

It's easy to slip into the mistake of speaking **REALLY QUICKLY** when you're giving a talk. Unfortunately this makes it harder for the audience to follow and gives you no time to breathe. Often, when giving a speech, you're speaking much faster than you think. An easy trick to avoid this is to count to three after you finish each point. Not only will this give you time to think, but it will also give the audience time to absorb what you have just said, and make you appear more calm and confident.

4 After the talk

It's likely that your audience will have lots of questions for you. Don't be daunted by this, and don't avoid them. Some of the best conversations happen during Q&A sessions, or just by talking to people after the event. It's also important to remember that there is nothing wrong with taking some time to think through your answer. This will help you to give a more thought-out response and show that you are taking their question seriously.

THE MOST IMPORTANT THING IS TO TRY TO RELAX AND ENJOY YOUR TALK. IT'LL BE OVER BEFORE YOU KNOW IT- SO MAKE THE MOST OF IT!

Dear Diary...

Talking at the United Nations

In December 2019, Ella and I were lucky enough to join four fellow young female activists at a Human Rights Conference called the **Young Activists Summit**. The event took place on Human Rights Day (10th December) — and we couldn't think of a better way to celebrate the day than by speaking in the Human Rights and Alliance of Civilizations Room of the United Nations in Geneva, where the summit took place!

We had the opportunity to talk alongside the other girls on a panel in front of a group of students aged 15–25 in the morning, and then to government officials in the afternoon. It was an **INCREDIBLE** (and, to be honest, nerve-racking) opportunity for us to stand up in front of some pretty important people and share our message. The other young women talking came from all around the globe, from Brazil to Iraq, each with an interesting, emotional and important story to tell.

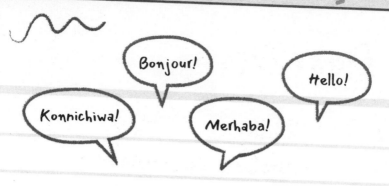

The UN certainly has a prestige, and for good reason! The venue was breathtaking, and it was fascinating to experience what everyone said being translated into at least four or five different languages. We had to wear earpieces that translated what people said in other languages into English!

As well as being in front of an audience in the UN, the event was broadcast live on Facebook, too. There were also numerous press interviews afterwards. **The conference aimed to help spread the messages that each of us activists brought from around the world.** It also aimed to form links between us all. We felt such an amazing sense of comradeship and support at the summit, and speaking to and hearing the stories of the other young activists was both humbling and inspiring.

We may have different causes, but in the end we all have the same goal to help **build a better world** and bring about change – change that can only happen if we all work together.

4

THE FUTURE

Now, it's not all doom and gloom when it comes to plastic. Luckily, there are some exciting things being done to help tackle the issue, through the actions of companies and even through science! Let's take a look...

Good VIBES

A greater number of organisations are thinking about the future and taking action to be more environmentally friendly. **FESTIVALS** attract millions of people to their sites every year, resulting in enormous amounts of plastic waste. Here are some festivals that are determined to improve the situation:

Yestival

Yestival holds a unique title – it's the **first ever Plastic Clever festival!** It started in 2015 and is all about spreading positivity and inspiration, making it the perfect first festival to get on board with the Plastic Clever initiative! No plastic cups are given out (tin mugs are available if you forget your own), all festival-goers are given a reusable bottle to fill from taps during the weekend, and all cutlery and plates are paper or wood. That's what we like to see!

Shambala

Shambala have an ambitious goal — to be single-use plastic free. Incredibly, they're practically there. They reduced the use of plastic bottles by banning their sale in 2014 and encourage the use of refillable ones instead. They've started a reusable cup scheme, where a small amount is paid for a cup at the bar, which you can trade for a clean one when you're done. They've put a tax on single-use coffee cups on site, and sell reusable coffee mugs for people to use if they don't have their own. They are also taking further steps to get rid of plastic from all areas of the festival, for example by using fewer plastic cable ties.

Glastonbury

Glastonbury is renowned for how big it is,
with hundreds of thousands of people
attending the music festival every year.
It's easy to imagine how much waste is generated
from an event this big – in 2017, festival-goers got through 1.3m plastic
bottles! Wow! Luckily, Glastonbury have started to reduce the
amount of plastic used. In 2019, they stopped the sale of plastic
bottles on-site and encouraged people to bring their own reusable
ones to refill. They also don't use plastic cups at bars, or plastic plates
and cutlery – some great steps in the right direction.

IF YOU WANT TO BE MORE PLASTIC CLEVER YOURSELF AT A FESTIVAL, REMEMBER TO TAKE YOUR OWN REUSABLE ITEMS TO USE DURING YOUR TIME THERE.

Also, **avoid glitter!** It looks lovely and shiny, but glitter is made
from plastic, meaning that when washed or brushed off it pollutes
the environment as a form of microplastics.

Dear Diary...

Speaking in parliament

Ella and I have been lucky enough to have been asked to speak at the Houses of Parliament on a few occasions now. However, when Greenpeace invited me to speak at an event they were hosting to announce their latest research on plastic pollution in UK rivers, I was the most nervous I'd been in a long time.

I was excited because I was going to meet one of my biggest inspirations – wildlife presenter **Steve Backshall**. But not only was I going to meet him, I was also going to speak alongside him! I couldn't believe it and had to keep pinching myself on the train down until it felt real.

I was also going to hear the research presented first-hand by Greenpeace's senior scientist **Dr David Santillo**, and get to chat with him about my research. This made me pretty excited too – and I don't care if that makes me sound a bit geeky! But why did I feel more nervous than usual?

Well, **Greenpeace had asked me to talk about my own research into plastic microfibres**. And as a budding scientist, I know my research is very DIY and not very scientifically robust. So, I was a bit worried that it might not be taken seriously at such a high-profile event.

I basically had two options:

1 Duck out of the opportunity and stick to talking about something more in my comfort zone.

2 Rise to the challenge and do my best!

Thankfully, I chose option 2 (as any aspiring activist should do, I suppose) and prepared as well as I could in the short space of time.

When the day of the event arrived, Steve Backshall inspired the room as only he can, Dr Santillo skilfully demonstrated the important role science can play in supporting a cause, and I enjoyed the opportunity of representing young people on an issue us kids are going to inherit.

Science and technology
TO THE RESCUE!

Can science and technology save us from our plastic pollution problem? Here are a few discoveries that may help us deal with the crisis by reducing the amount of waste plastic or supplying a nature-friendly alternative.

Magic enzyme

In 2016, Japanese scientists found a type of bacterium living in a rubbish dump that could break down PET, the type of plastic used to make soft drink bottles, into its original ingredients. The bacteria had evolved this ability to use the plastic as a source of food.

Scientists in the UK studied the enzyme in the bacterium – named **Ideonella sakaiensis** – that let it break down the plastic. Enzymes are proteins made by living things to speed up chemical reactions that otherwise would take a much longer time to occur.

Yum!

During an experiment to try to understand how the new plastic-chomping enzyme evolved in the bacterium, the team accidentally made a version of the enzyme that was even more effective at breaking down PET! This discovery means that we could build factories that use the enzyme to break down the millions of plastic bottles polluting the world. The ingredients could then be used to make new bottles, rather than using more oil drilled from the ground.

Fantastic fungus

Scientists have also discovered that a fungus living in a rubbish dump in Pakistan, called **Aspergillus tubingensis**, has evolved enzymes that let it eat the plastic polyurethane. This mutant fungus could be used in a controlled way in other dumps. However, some people worry that it might spread outside the dumps and become an invasive species, causing damage to the environment.

Awesome algae

Algae, which are simple plant-like living things, can be used to make biodegradable water bottles, which break down soon after use. In 2016, Icelandic product designer Ari Jónsson used water and red algae powder to make a material that could be moulded into water bottles. Water inside the bottles may take on a slight taste of the algae after a few days – and if you like this flavour, it's safe to eat the bottle as well!

Crude dude

Japanese inventor Akinori Ito has invented an oil-producing machine that converts waste plastic into oil, which can be used as fuel, reducing the need to take oil from underground. The machine can use 60% of all types of plastic, and it produces about 1 litre (1.75 UK pints) of oil from 1 kg (2.2lb) of plastic. Ito's appliance is very expensive but he hopes to bring the price down so that one day every household can afford one.

Dear Diary...

Our TV presenting debut!

FYI is a news programme on Sky that aims to engage young people in current affairs. It's presented by kids, for kids, and Ella was lucky enough to be selected as one of the original four presenters.

> **Nothing lucky about it Amy...**

Now, as a committed campaigner against single-use plastics, Ella took on the role of **"the environmental one"** in the team. So, as plastic pollution stories hit the news – as they do quite regularly – she is able to present them with confidence and authority. Her position on FYI has been fantastic for raising awareness of Kids Against Plastic.

One highlight for Kids Against Plastic on FYI was when Ella and I were filmed trying to have a **PLASTIC-FREE DAY**.

It was good fun but very challenging. As you'll know, we prefer to encourage people to be **Plastic Clever** – and use plastic wisely – rather than plastic free, because that is virtually impossible. Anyway, we gave it a shot. These were some of our interesting findings...

• We had terrible bed hair (!!) because we couldn't use our hairbrushes, due to their plastic handles. This wasn't helped by not being able to use a hair dryer!
• We had to walk everywhere – most transport had plastic in it. Sore legs all round.
• We enjoyed the smell of home-baked bread – no prepackaged sliced bread allowed.
• The best thing, though, was seeing Ella's tongue when she used charcoal 'tooth tabs' instead of toothpaste!

The point of the programme was to demonstrate how much we rely on plastic and how difficult it is to go without it.

AFTER THAT EXPERIENCE, WE DEFINITELY STILL RECOMMEND TRYING TO BE PLASTIC CLEVER AS A STARTING POINT!

TIME TO ACT

You may have gathered from the book that us kids are in a bit of a pickle. According to some of the clever people at the UN, we need to stop the Earth warming by 1.5°C, or we will see **even more** disastrous effects of climate change. If the Earth warms by 2°C, the sea will rise higher, almost all coral will be at great risk, and there'll be no ice in the Arctic once every ten years instead of once every hundred years. In order to stop this, we need urgent climate action – **now**. The UN say that we need to take global action to help the planet by 2030, which doesn't give us long! **Now, this can be pretty scary.** The effects that climate change will have on the planet will be terrible, as is the global lack of action when it comes to dealing with it.

Where has all the ice gone?

BUT, as we've seen through this book, we need to remember that we can all be part of tackling tricky problems and making a difference.

We don't need to wait for world leaders to act before we all do something.

HELP

YOUTH 4 EARTH

PEACE

THE TIME FOR CHANGE IS NOW

We can't let the voice of the youth go to waste. We're more powerful than we think! We shouldn't let our age hold us back, or listen to adults who tell us we don't understand. We need to stand up for what we believe in, for our generation's future, and for our children's.

REMEMBER – IT DOESN'T MATTER WHAT YOU DO TO MAKE A POSITIVE DIFFERENCE, JUST DO SOMETHING.

Whether that's making your school Plastic Clever, doing a weekly litter pick or just stopping using plastic bottles, the important thing is to start now. Not at the weekend. Not next week, or next month. **NOW!**

We hope that this book has helped you to realise the scale of the issues facing our planet, but also given you the belief that you can have a positive impact.

165

5

GET STARTED!

So, you want to make a difference – you now have the knowhow, but what next? It can be hard to know how to start campaigning, so here are a few useful questionnaires, quizzes, and resources to help you find your (activist) feet.

ACTIVIST QUESTIONNAIRE

Want to be the next global changemaker? Grab a pen and piece of paper and fill in this questionnaire to get started.

When it comes to making a change, what is your passion?

What is your main concern?

What will your solution be?

(Think BIG! Your solution can be as creative or ambitious as you want.)

What will be your first actions to tackle the problem?

What can you do tomorrow?

(What small actions can you take to make a difference quickly?)

How can you share your story? Who will you get to help you?

Which tools will you use?

(What do you need to make your action plan work? This could be litter pickers for collecting plastic, or poster board to make signs.)

169

ACTIVISTS' FAQ

You might find that you'll get asked similar questions every time you do talks, or Q&A sessions. Here are some of the ones that we get asked a lot, if you want a handy answer to fall back on!

> ## Why is it important to tackle plastic pollution?

> From the perspective of the younger generation, it's important that we take action to address plastic pollution – and **NOW!** Plastic pollution is going to outlive us, and it's a problem that my generation and our children's generation are going to inherit unless we all take urgent action to reduce our plastic usage now.

Why do you think young people should get involved in environmental issues?

We think that young people should get involved in any projects that they are passionate about, because of the power that the youth voice can have. If we want change to happen, we have to make it happen! Standing up for what you believe in is so important, particularly as these are issues that we are going to inherit as we get older. If you want to see a change being made, you can't sit back and let others do the work.

What can I do to tackle plastic pollution?

People really underestimate the impact that small, everyday actions can have. Tackling plastic pollution doesn't have to mean going completely plastic-free immediately – something that is expensive and practically impossible for most people. We encourage people to be more **"Plastic Clever"** instead, and to try to refuse four items as a start – plastic cups, straws, bottles, and bags. Start small, but do something – that's the most important thing.

FAKE or FACT?

Did these things really happen, or are they completely fake? Test your knowledge with this quiz. If you've been reading carefully, you may already know some of the answers!

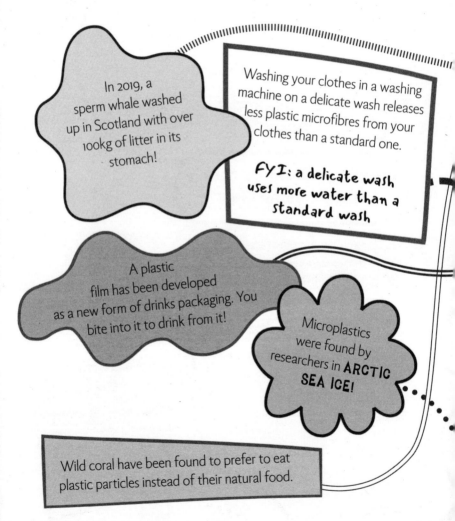

In 2019, a sperm whale washed up in Scotland with over 100kg of litter in its stomach!

Washing your clothes in a washing machine on a delicate wash releases less plastic microfibres from your clothes than a standard one.

FYI: a delicate wash uses more water than a standard wash

A plastic film has been developed as a new form of drinks packaging. You bite into it to drink from it!

Microplastics were found by researchers in ARCTIC SEA ICE!

Wild coral have been found to prefer to eat plastic particles instead of their natural food.

FACT!

Not only is this correct, but even more awful is the fact that these plastic pieces carry bacteria that can sicken or even kill the coral!

FACT!

And this isn't the first time this has happened – another whale was found in 2019 with **40kg of plastic** in its stomach, while a sperm whale was found in Indonesia in 2018 with more than 1,000 pieces of plastic inside it. **Yuck!**

FAKE!

The truth is actually much better – a company called Skipping Rocks Lab developed **Oooho** capsules, bubble-like pouches that are made from a **SEAWEED** membrane that you can drink from and swallow! They were used at the 2019 London Marathon instead of plastic water bottles – a great way to reduce plastic usage. Unlike plastic, the seaweed film will biodegrade in six weeks if dropped on the floor.

FAKE!

Delicate washes cause clothes to shed more microfibres than standard washes. Researchers think that this is due to a higher volume of water being used. This is forced through the clothing, causing fibres to wash out.

FACT!

Sadly this is true. Microplastics have also been found in tap water, remote mountain ranges like the Rocky Mountains and Pyrenees, and even in the air we breathe!

Test your
KNOWLEDGE!

Time to see if you're a plastic brainbox! We're sure you've been **reading very carefully**, so if this is too easy, test your friends or family instead.

1: What type of plastic are **single-use water bottles** made from?

2: What is the **harmful chemical** that used to be in plastic, which is thought to be harmful to our bodies?

3: On average, how long does it take a **plastic bag to break down** when it is thrown away?

4: What percentage of **clothing** is made from material containing plastic?

5: What are **bioplastics** made from?

6: How many **sea birds are killed** by plastic in the oceans every year?

7: What percentage of global energy is **non-renewable**?

8: How many people are estimated to have taken part in the **September 2019 Earth Strike**?

ANSWERS:

Q1 PET Q2 BPA Q3 15–20 years Q4 60%
Q5 Organic/plant material (such as food waste or wood chippings) Q6 1 million Q7 80% Q8 4 million

Interview with...
AMY

Let's learn a little more about Amy from Kids Against Plastic...

Q: WHAT DO YOU WANT TO DO WHEN YOU'RE OLDER?
A: Be an environmental activist! I would love to carry on campaigning into the future – now that I've found out about all the ways we're damaging our planet, I don't think I can ever turn my back on trying to protect it.

Q: IF THERE WAS ONE THING YOU COULD TAKE TO A DESERT ISLAND, WHAT WOULD IT BE?
A: A multi-tool – I think a knife and mini saw would come in handy for some emergency bushcraft.

Q: WHAT'S YOUR FAVOURITE BOOK? (EXCEPT FOR THIS ONE!)
A: *Pride and Prejudice* by Jane Austen.

Q: WHAT'S THE MOST ANNOYING THING ABOUT ELLA?
A: She's a little stubborn, something that can be both good and bad!

Q: WHAT DO YOU MOST ADMIRE ABOUT ELLA?
A: She's always there to talk to, she's my best friend in a lot of ways. She's amazingly determined – when Ella sets her mind on something, you can't stop her. It makes her the perfect campaigning buddy!

Q: IF YOU COULD MEET ONE PERSON FROM HISTORY, WHO WOULD IT BE?
A: Eleanor Roosevelt – she stood up for what she believed in, and used her position as First Lady for good.

Q: WHAT DO YOU THINK SHOULD BE TAUGHT IN SCHOOLS THAT CURRENTLY ISN'T?
A: I think it would be good to have a greater focus on the environment – climate change and other environmental problems shouldn't be things that are just touched on in science or geography lessons. In order for us to be engaged with and protecting the world we live in, we first need to understand and care for it, and school is the perfect place to start.

Q: IF YOU WERE ENVIRONMENT SECRETARY, WHAT WOULD BE YOUR FIRST ACTION?
A: Put a tax on plastic production by large corporations. There's no way we can justify producing billions of plastic items like bottles every day, and I think that some of the big producers of plastic need to start taking responsibility for the impact they're having.

Q: WHAT'S YOUR FAVOURITE SPORT OR OUTDOOR ACTIVITY?
A: Rock climbing!

Q: WHICH SONG WOULD YOU CHOOSE AS THE BACKGROUND MUSIC TO YOUR LIFE?
A: "Simple As This" by Jake Bugg. It's a song that means a lot to my family, as well as being the first one I learnt on the guitar! Jake Bugg is also from Nottingham, like us.

Interview with...
ELLA

Now it's Ella's turn to tell us a bit about herself.

Q: WHAT DO YOU WANT TO DO WHEN YOU'RE OLDER?
A: I would like to do TV presenting all around the world or be an environmental lawyer – I haven't decided yet!

Q: IF THERE WAS ONE THING YOU COULD TAKE TO A DESERT ISLAND, WHAT WOULD IT BE?
A: Not to be classic, but a raft I guess!

Q: WHAT'S YOUR FAVOURITE BOOK?
(EXCEPT FOR THIS ONE!)
A: Ooooh a book I really enjoyed is *The Tattooist of Auschwitz* by Heather Morris – it's a gripping and thought-provoking story that is based on real history.

Q: WHAT'S THE MOST ANNOYING THING ABOUT AMY?
A: Amy annoys me when she's a know-it-all and when she makes fun of me :(

Q: WHAT DO YOU MOST ADMIRE ABOUT AMY?
A: How good she is at everything in school – she is soooo smart!

Q: IF YOU COULD MEET ONE PERSON FROM HISTORY, WHO WOULD IT BE?

A: I would have loved to meet Emmeline Pankhurst from the suffragette movement who fought for women's equality. She's a huge inspiration for standing up for what she believed in and she helped get women the amount of equality they have today.

Q: WHAT DO YOU THINK SHOULD BE TAUGHT IN SCHOOLS THAT CURRENTLY ISN'T?

A: I think kids in schools should be taught about all of the different problems in the world, so they have more awareness of what's happening and what they can do about it. As the future generation we need to know what's happening to the planet we'll inherit so we can make a difference before it's too late.

Q: IF YOU WERE ENVIRONMENT SECRETARY, WHAT WOULD BE YOUR FIRST ACTION?

A: As environment secretary I would come up with a tax for plastic items to discourage people from buying it as consumer demand is what brings about change.

Q: WHAT'S YOUR FAVOURITE SPORT OR OUTDOOR ACTIVITY?

A: I enjoy dancing – I find it expressive and fun.

Q: WHICH SONG WOULD YOU CHOOSE AS THE BACKGROUND MUSIC TO YOUR LIFE?

A: "My Shot" from *Hamilton*. It's an amazing musical with incredible songs that I love and this one is about not missing your chance to make a change.

Useful RESOURCES

Whether you want to help your school reduce their plastic usage or find out more about plastic and the issues it causes, here are a few resources you might find useful:

We've put together a bank of resources to help you out:

kidsagainstplastic.co.uk/learn

The **STORY OF STUFF** make animated videos to help you understand environmental and social issues. They're really fun to watch, and there's plenty about plastic – **make sure you check them out!**

storyofstuff.org

THE MARINE CONSERVATION SOCIETY have some great resources to use for beach cleans, including survey forms to accurately record what you pick up.

mcsuk.org/beachwatch/ resources

www.

For British-based activists, **Keep Britain Tidy's Eco schools programme** have some resources you might find useful at school!

www.eco-schools. org.uk/resources

World Oceans Day happens every year on the 8th June, and the **We Are Ocean** collective have put together loads of resources for schools to get involved. They include films and slides for assemblies, activity packs, and stories to inspire a love for the oceans.

worldoceanday.school

Emily Penn (see pages 96–97) has put together an awesome toolkit to help you combat plastic pollution. It's the perfect place to go if you're looking for some more insight or knowledge into tackling plastic, and how to go about it.

oceanchangemakers.com

Keep on top of the latest news at the BBC website **PLASTICS WATCH**.

www.bbc.co.uk/programmes/ articles/11CnCQRoGJfkDgJs57sR5Ps/war-on-plastic

Incredible Oceans make studying the ocean... **well, incredible!**

incredibleoceans.org

GLOSSARY

Biodegradable: describes something that breaks down naturally in the environment

Bioplastic: plastic that has been made from natural plant materials (for example wood chippings or food waste)

BPA: a chemical used to make hard plastics, like water bottles. It is thought to be really bad for our health, so its use has been restricted in many countries around the world

Carbon cycle: a natural cycle of what happens to carbon in nature. It involves almost all life on Earth!

Carbon dioxide: a greenhouse gas made of carbon and oxygen. It occurs naturally in the atmosphere, but levels are now rising

Carbon footprint: the amount of carbon dioxide released into the atmosphere by the activities of one person or a group of people

Climate change: a change in general weather conditions over a large area, such as planet Earth. Earth's climate has always changed naturally over time but this process is now speeding up

Compostable plastics: plastics that break down in controlled conditions in an industrial composter

Disposable: describes something that is only used once before being thrown away

Downcycling: where plastic is made into items of lower quality than the original product (for example, plastic bottles being made into a fleece)

Fossil fuels: resources that are made up of the remains of dead plants and animals, such as oil or natural gas. Burning fossil fuels is one of the leading causes of climate change

Garbage patches: rubbish in the oceans that has been brought together by ocean currents into giant floating patches. The largest of these is the Great Pacific Garbage Patch in the North Pacific Ocean

Global warming: an increase in global temperature due to increased greenhouse gas levels

Greenhouse gases: gases in the Earth's atmosphere that absorb the Sun's radiation. Carbon dioxide and methane are greenhouse gases

Gyres: Large scale surface ocean currents that move around in a circle, collecting pieces of rubbish into garbage patches

LED light bulb: a source of light that uses significantly less energy than traditional light bulbs

Microplastics: pieces of plastic under 5mm in size. They can be in the form of nurdles, fragments of larger plastic items, or as microfibres from our clothing

PET: one of the most common types of plastic, used to make plastic bottles and jars for spreads and sauces

Plastic microfibres: a form of microplastics – tiny plastic threads less than 5mm in size that wash out of our clothes every time we put them in the washing machine. They are often made of polyester or acrylic (types of plastic)

Power plant: a facility where electric power is generated, using fuels such as coal and natural gas

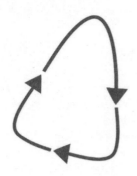

Recycling: the process of turning something into a new object

Renewable: a resource that does not run out. Renewable energy comes from a source that is never depleted, such as wind or solar energy

Sustainable: use of resources in a way that ensures they will not run out or become difficult to find

The Sustainable Development Goals: 17 ambitious world goals devised by the United Nations, backed by countries around the world, calling for world leaders to work together to tackle big global issues

The United Nations: an international organization with nearly 200 member states that aims to develop friendly relations between countries

United Nations Environment Programme: a global environment authority that helps implement policies to support the environment in United Nations countries

INDEX

A few thank yous from Amy

Before you start the process of writing a book, you really don't understand the amount of work that goes into the finished package – not just the writing, but everything else behind the scenes. So, I can't thank the awesome team at DK enough for supporting me along this journey.

I have to say a big thank you to my amazing family, who put up with reading all of my initial first drafts and put their earplugs to good use for all the excited screaming when illustrations and cover designs came through.

And, thank you to all of the other young activists, both those included in this book and the many, many others working tirelessly for their cause around the world. You set me on this journey, and I only hope that many other young people will follow.

The publisher would like to thank

Helen Augello Miles for proofreading; Helen Peters for the index; Anne Damerell and Nishani Reed for legal advice; Steve Backshall and all of the amazing interviewees; Tim and Kerry Meek for your constant support; and Lauren Gardner at Bell Lomax Moreton for introducing us to Amy and Ella.

Most of all thank you to Amy and Ella – you've been a joy to work with throughout!